Gourmet Desserts Made Simple

Impressive Yet Easy Recipes

By

Marie H. Sanders

CHEESE

Cheese should not be tightly covered. When it becomes dry and hard, grate and keep covered until ready to use. It may be added to starchy foods.

Care should be exercised in planning meals in which cheese is employed as a substitute for meat. As cheese dishes are inclined to be somewhat "heavy," they should be offset by crisp, watery vegetables, water cress, celery, lettuce, fruit salads and light desserts, preferably fresh or cooked fruit. Another point, too, is to be considered. Whether raw or cooked, cheese seems to call for the harder kinds of bread--crusty rolls or biscuits, zwieback, toast, pulled bread or hard crackers.

A soft, crumbly cheese is best for cooking.

Cheese is sufficiently cooked when melted, if cooked longer it becomes tough and leathery.

Baking-soda in cheese dishes which are cooked makes the casein more digestible.

COTTAGE CHEESE (POT CHEESE)

Heat sour milk slowly until the whey rises to the top; pour it off, put the curd in a bag and let it dry for six hours without squeezing it.
Pour it into a bowl and break it fine with a wooden spoon. Season with salt. Mold into balls and keep in a cool place. It is best when fresh.

KOCH KAESE (BOILED CHEESE)

Press one quart of fine cottage cheese through a coarse sieve or colander and set it away in a cool place for a week, stirring it once or twice during that time; when it has become quite strong, stir it smooth with a wooden or silver spoon; add a saltspoon of salt and one-fourth as much of caraway seed, yolks of two eggs and an even tablespoon of flour which has been previously dissolved in about one-half cup of cold milk; stir the flour and milk until it is a smooth paste, adding a lump of butter, about the size of an egg; add all to the cheese. Put the cheese on to boil until quite thick; stirring occasionally; boil altogether about one-half hour, stirring constantly the last ten minutes; the cheese must look smooth as velvet. Pour it into a dish which has been previously rinsed in cold water. Set it away in a cool place; to keep it any length of time, cover it with a clean cloth which has been dipped in and wrung out of beer. This cheese is excellent for rye bread sandwiches.

A DELICIOUS CREAM CHEESE

Sweet milk is allowed to stand until it is like a jelly, but does not separate. Then it is poured into a cheese-cloth bag and hung up to drain until all the water is out of it and only the rich creamy substance remains. Sometimes it takes from twelve to twenty-four hours. At the end of this time the cheese is turned from the bag into a bowl; then to every pint of the cheesy substance a tablespoon of butter is added and enough salt to season it palatably. Then it is whipped up with a fork until it is a smooth paste and enough put on a plate to make a little brick, like a Philadelphia cheese. With two knives, one in each hand, lightly press the cheese together in the shape of a brick, smooth it over the top and put it away to cool. One quart of rich sour milk will make a good sized cheese.

CHEESE BALLS, No. 1

Take one cake of cream cheese, one-quarter of a pound of chopped figs, one-quarter of a pound of chopped walnuts, roll into balls and serve on lettuce leaves.

CHEESE BALLS, No. 2

Mix one cake Neufchatel cheese, a piece of butter the size of the cheese, one tablespoon of cream, one-quarter teaspoon of salt and six dashes of Tabasco Sauce and form one large ball or several small ones and roll in chopped pecan nuts.

CHEESE SOUFFLE

Dissolve one and one-half tablespoons of butter, add one tablespoon of flour, stir until it loosens from the pan; add one and one-half cups of rich milk, pepper and salt. Take from the fire, add gradually four egg yolks and three-quarters of a cup of grated cheese, then the stiffly beaten whites of eggs. Bake in a hot oven in china ramekins about fifteen minutes and serve immediately.

CHEESE TIMBALS FOR TWELVE PEOPLE

Take one pint of milk, four tablespoons of flour, and use enough of the milk to dissolve the flour, the balance put in double boiler; when it boils, add the dissolved flour, then add one-quarter pound imported Swiss cheese grated. Let these two boil for fifteen minutes; when cool, add the yolks of four eggs; drop one in at a time and beat, then strain through a fine sieve about ten minutes before you put in the pans; beat the whites of two eggs and put in the above and mix; grease timbal forms, fill three-quarters full only; bake in pan of boiling water twenty minutes. Let them stand about two minutes, turn out on little plates, and serve with tomato sauce, a sprig of parsley put on top of each one.

WELSH RAREBIT

Melt one tablespoon of butter, add two cups finely cut American cheese, when it melts add one-half cup of milk or stale beer, keep stirring until it is smooth. Add one-half teaspoon of English mustard, two beaten eggs. Cook one minute longer and salt to taste. Serve on toast.

GOLDEN BUCK

One pound of cheese, one-eighth pound of butter, one-half glass of ale, one teaspoon of mustard, one egg (well beaten), and salt and paprika.
Put butter in pan, and when melted add cheese cut up or grated; stir, and as cheese melts, add ale. When it begins to bubble, add egg well beaten. Stir continually to keep from getting stringy. In two or three minutes it will be ready to serve. Pour over hot buttered toast. This quantity is sufficient for four persons.

CHEESE BREAD

Take six thick slices of stale bread, well buttered; cut them in two; dip into milk; then place in a baking dish, with alternating layers of thinly sliced cheese, having cheese for top. Add half a cup of milk, into which a half teaspoon of dry mustard has been put. Bake in quick oven fifteen minutes. Serve at once.

GREEN CORN, TOMATOES AND CHEESE

Into one tablespoon of melted butter stir two cups of grated cheese until it, too, is melted. Add three-quarters of a cup of canned or grated fresh corn, one ripe green pepper, stir them, add one egg yolk mixed with one-half cup of tomato puree, one teaspoon of salt, one-half teaspoon of paprika. Toast five slices of bread and pour this mixture over it. Serve hot.

RICE AND CHEESE

Melt two ounces of butter in a stew-pan; fry in the buttery finely minced onion. When this is of a nice golden color stir into it a quarter of a pound of well-boiled rice. Work it well with a fork and then pour all into a buttered pie dish. Dredge over with a good coating of grated cheese, sprinkle the surface with melted butter and bake until nicely browned.

MACARONI AND CHEESE

Break three ounces of macaroni--noodles or spaghetti answer equally well--into small pieces, boil in rapidly boiling salted water; when tender drain off the water and add half a pint of milk; cook slowly till the macaroni has absorbed most of the milk. To half a pint of thick white sauce add two ounces of grated cheese and mix with the macaroni; last of all add two well-beaten eggs. Butter a pudding mold, sprinkle it with browned bread crumbs and pour in the macaroni mixture; steam gently for about half an hour, turn out and fill the centre with stewed tomatoes and mushrooms.

CHEESE OMELET

Cook in double boiler one cup of milk, add one tablespoon of butter, one tablespoon of flour blended together and cook till thick; one cup of cheese cut up added, and stir till dissolved. Remove from fire and stir in yolks of four eggs beaten, one-half teaspoon of salt (pepper). Fold in whites of four eggs beaten stiff and a pinch of baking powder. Bake in a buttered dish one-half hour.

CHEESE AND SWEET GREEN PEPPERS

Cheese and peppers make a very nice combination. Melt two ounces of cheese, add a tablespoon of chopped peppers and the same amount of butter, a little paprika, salt, and if liked, mustard. When the ingredients have been well blended pour the mixture on hot buttered toast and serve.

CHEESE FONDUE

Soak one-half cup of bread crumbs in one scant cup of milk; dissolve a speck of bicarbonate of soda in a drop of hot water and add to the milk, one egg, yolk and white beaten separately, one-half cup of dry cheese grated, one tablespoon of butter, salt and pepper to taste, beat well, pour into a well buttered baking dish, strew dry crumbs moistened with butter over the top, and bake in a hot oven until light brown. Serve at once in the dish in which it is baked.

TOMATOES, EGGS AND CHEESE (HUNGARIAN STYLE)

Place two tablespoons of butter in a pan (after having the water boil to heat the pan). Let butter melt, add one small onion chopped fine and cook until soft, a pint of tomatoes strained and let come to a boil; add one-half pound mild cheese cut fine; and stir until smooth. Break in three eggs and stir hard until eggs are done. Serve on buttered toast.

CRACKERS AND CHEESE

Split in two some Bent's water biscuits; moisten them with hot water and pour over each piece a little melted butter and French mustard; then spread with a thick layer of grated cheese; sprinkle with paprika or cayenne. Place them in a hot oven until the cheese is soft and creamy.

RAMEKINS OF EGG AND CHEESE

Beat three new-laid eggs and blend thoroughly with two ounces of grated cheese and one ounce of partly melted butter. Place the mixture in little pans or saucers and bake in the oven.

BREAD

Home-made bread is very much more palatable and more nutritious than baker's bread and it is worth while to spend time and effort in its preparation.

To make good bread, it is necessary to have good flour, fresh yeast and the liquid used in moistening must be neither too hot nor too cold or the bread will not rise properly.

FLOUR

The housekeeper should know about the different kinds of flour. We get the bread flour from the spring wheat; the pastry flour from the winter wheat.

Bread flour contains more gluten than pastry flour and is used for bread on that account. Pastry flour having less gluten and slightly more starch is more suitable for pastry and cake mixtures and is used wherever softness and lightness are desired.

Graham flour is the whole kernel of wheat ground.

Entire wheat flour is the flour resulting from the grinding of all but the outer layer of the wheat.

Rye flour is next best to wheat flour for bread making, but is generally combined with wheat flour, since by itself it makes a sticky bread.

Cornmeal is also combined with wheat flour.

Variety bread is composed of bread flour, rye flour and cornmeal combined in one loaf.

If flour is musty; it is not kosher and must be destroyed. Keep flour either in tins or barrels in a dry atmosphere.

YEAST

In cities where fresh compressed yeast can be obtained, it is not worth while to prepare one's own.

Compressed yeast is always in proper condition to use until it becomes soft, often the yeast cakes are slightly discolored, but this does not affect the yeast, being caused by the oxidation of the starch in the cake.

Keep yeast in cool place.

HOME MADE YEAST

Grate six large raw potatoes, have ready a gallon of water in which you have boiled one and one-half cups of hops. Strain through a fine hair sieve, boiling hot, over the potatoes, stirring well, or the mixture will thicken like starch. Add a scant cup of sugar and one-half cup of salt. When cold, add a yeast cake or a cup of fresh yeast. Let it stand until a thick foam rises on the top. Bottle in a few days. If kept in a cool place, this yeast will last a long time. Use one cup of yeast for one large baking. In making yeast, from time to time, use a cup of the same with which to start the new yeast.

One cup of liquid yeast is equal to one cake of compressed yeast.

When yeast is not obtainable to start the fermentation in making yeast, mix a thin batter of flour and water, and let it stand in a warm place until it is full of bubbles. This ferment has only half the strength of yeast so double the amount must be used.

TO MAKE BREAD

Try the yeast always by setting to raise in a cup of lukewarm water or milk, if you use compressed yeast add salt and sugar.

If it rises in the course of ten or fifteen minutes, the yeast is fit to use. In making bread always use sifted flour. Set a sponge with lukewarm milk or water, keeping it covered in a warm place until very light, then mold this sponge by adding flour, until very light into one large ball, then knead well and steadily for twenty minutes. Set to rise again in a warm place free from drafts, and when it has risen to double its former bulk, take a knife, cut through the dough in several places, then place this dough on a baking board which has been sprinkled with flour. Work with the palm of the hand, always kneading towards the centre of the ball (the dough must rebound like a rubber ball). When this leaves the board and the hands perfectly clean the dough may be formed into loaves or rolls.

Place in pan, greased slightly with a good oil, let rise until the imprint of the finger does not remain, and bake.

The oven for baking bread should be hot enough to brown a teaspoon of flour in five minutes.

If baked in a coal range, the fire must be just the proper heat so as not to have to add fuel or shake the stove.

If baked in a gas range, light oven to full heat five minutes before putting the bread in the oven, and bake in a moderately hot oven forty-five minutes, unless the loaves are very large when one hour will be the proper time.

When taken from the oven, the bread may be wrapped in a clean towel wrung out of warm water (this prevents the crust from becoming hard); place bread in slanting position or allow it to cool on a wire rack.

WHITE BREAD

Set the dough at night and bake early in the morning; take one-half cake of compressed yeast, set in a cup of lukewarm milk or water adding a teaspoon of salt and a tablespoon of sugar. Let this rise, if it does not, the yeast is not fresh or good. Measure eight cups of sifted flour into a deep bread bowl, add one teaspoon of salt; make a depression in the centre, pour in the risen yeast and one cup of lukewarm milk or water. In winter be sure that the bowl, flour, milk, in fact everything has been thoroughly warmed before mixing. Mix the dough slowly with a wooden spoon and then knead as directed.

This amount will make two loaves, either twisted or in small bread pans. Bake forty-five minutes in a moderate oven.

If the bread is set in the morning use a cake of compressed yeast and bake the loaves in the afternoon.

INDIVIDUAL LOAVES

Make dough according to the above recipe. Work small pieces of dough into strands a finger long, and take three strands for each loaf. Make small as possible, brush with beaten egg; or sweetened water and sprinkle with poppy seed (mohn). Allow them to rise before setting them in the oven. These are called "Vienna loaves" and are used at weddings, parties and for the Succoth festival in the Succah.

If one-half cake of yeast has been used, the half cake of yeast which is left over, can be kept in good condition several days by rewrapping it in the tinfoil and keeping it in a cool, dry place.

BUTTERBARCHES

Dissolve one cake of compressed yeast in one-half cup of lukewarm milk, add a teaspoon of salt, and a tablespoon of sugar and let it rise. Then make a soft dough of eight cups of sifted flour and as much milk as is required to work it, about two cups; add the yeast, one-half cup of sugar, four tablespoons of butter dissolved in the warm milk, the grated peel of a lemon, two or three dozen raisins seeded, and two eggs well beaten. Work this dough perfectly smooth with the palm of your hand, adding more flour if necessary. It is hardly possible to tell the exact amount of flour to use; experience will teach you when you have added enough. Different brands of flour vary, some being drier than others.
Work the dough as directed, set it aside covered until it is double the bulk of the original piece of dough. Then work again and divide the dough into two parts, and divide each of the pieces of dough into three parts. Work the six pieces of dough thoroughly and then roll each piece into a long strand; three

of which are to be longer than the other three. Braid the three long strands into one braid (should be thicker in the centre than at the end), and braid the shorter strands into one braid and lay it on, top of the long braid, pressing the ends together.

Butter a long baking-pan, lift the barches into the pan and set in a warm place to rise again for about one-half hour. Then brush the top with beaten egg and sprinkle poppy seed all over the top. Bake in a moderate oven one hour.

BARCHES

These are to be used for a meat meal and are made in the same manner as butter barches, omitting the milk and butter; use water and a little shortening of dripping or rendered fat or a vegetable oil; grate a dozen almonds (blanched) and add with two well-beaten eggs, one-half cup of sugar, salt, raisins and the grated peel of one lemon. Work just as you would butter barches. Bake one hour in moderate oven. Wrap in a damp, clean towel as soon as baked to prevent the crust from becoming too hard.

POTATO BREAD

Add one medium-sized mashed boiled potato to any of the foregoing recipes. This will give a more moist bread, which retains its freshness longer.

GRAHAM BREAD

Dissolve one cake of compressed yeast and four tablespoons of light brown sugar or molasses in one cup of lukewarm water and one cup of milk which has been scalded and cooled to lukewarm. Add two tablespoons of melted butter, then four cups of Graham flour and one cup of white flour (sifted), adding flour gradually, and one teaspoon of salt. Knead thoroughly, being sure to keep dough soft. Cover and set aside in a warm place to rise for about two hours. When double in bulk, turn out on kneading board, mold into loaves, and place in well-greased pans, cover and set to rise again-- about one hour or until light. Bake one hour, in a slower oven than for white bread. If wanted for overnight use one-half cake of yeast and an extra half teaspoon of salt.

GLUTEN BREAD

Dissolve one cake of compressed yeast and one tablespoon of sugar in one cup of milk, scalded and cooled, and one cup of lukewarm water; add one level tablespoon of butter then three cups of gluten flour gradually, and one teaspoon of salt. Knead thoroughly until smooth and elastic; place in well-greased bowl; cover and set aside in a warm place, free from draught, to rise until light, which should be in about two hours.
Mold into loaves; place in greased pans, filling them half full. Cover, let rise again, and when double in bulk, which should be in about one hour, bake in moderate oven forty-five minutes.

This will make two one-pound loaves. For diet use omit shortening and sugar.

RAISIN BREAD

Make dough as directed for Butterbarches, using one-quarter cup of raisins and omitting the lemon and egg. Form in loaves, fill well-greased pans half full; cover and let rise until light; about one hour. Glaze with egg diluted with water, and bake forty-five minutes.

ROLLED OATS BREAD

Pour two cups of boiling water over two cups of rolled oats, cover and let stand until lukewarm. Dissolve one cake of compressed yeast and one-fourth cup of brown sugar in one-half cup of lukewarm water, add two tablespoons of shortening, the oatmeal and the water in which it has been swelling. Beat well, add about three cups of flour to make a dough, also add one teaspoon of salt. Let rise until it doubles in bulk. Mold into two loaves in pan and bake forty-five minutes.

POTATO-RYE BREAD

Cook one quart of potatoes diced, in boiling water until tender. Strain, reserving potato water. Measure and add enough more water to make three cups. Let come to a boil, add one-quarter cup of salt, and very gradually one

and one-quarter cups of cornmeal. Cook two minutes, stirring constantly until thick. Remove from fire, add two tablespoons of any kind of fat, the potatoes riced or mashed and when cooled two cups of flour; then one tablespoon of sugar and one cake of yeast dissolved in one cup of lukewarm water. Mix and knead to a stiff dough adding wheat flour to keep it from sticking. Cover, set aside in a warm place overnight, or until double its bulk. Shape into four loaves, let rise again; bake in a moderate oven one hour or more, until well done.
Glaze with egg diluted with water before putting in the oven. These loaves will keep moist one week.

RYE BREAD (AMERICAN) No. 1

Dissolve one cake compressed yeast in two cups of lukewarm water and one cup of milk which has been scalded and cooled; or if so desired the milk may be omitted and all water used; add two and one-half cups of rye flour or enough to make a sponge. Beat well; cover and set aside in a warm place, free from draught, to rise about two hours. When light add one and one-half cups of sifted white flour, one tablespoon of melted butter or oil, two and one-half cups of rye flour to make a soft dough and last one tablespoon of salt. Turn on a board and knead or pound it five minutes. Place in greased bowl; cover and let rise until double in bulk--about two hours. Turn on board and shape into loaves; place in floured shallow pans; cover and let rise again until light--about one hour. Brush with white of egg and water, to glaze. With sharp knife cut lightly three strokes diagonally across top, and place in oven. Bake in slower oven than for white bread. Caraway seeds may be used if desired.

By adding one-half cup of sour dough, left from previous baking, an acid flavor is obtained, which is considered by many a great improvement.
This should be added to the sponge.

RYE BREAD, No. 2

Sift three cups of rye flour, three cups of wheat flour and two teaspoons of salt in a bowl. Dissolve one-half cake of compressed yeast or any other yeast in two cups of lukewarm water. When the yeast is dissolved pour it into the flour and make into a dough. Lay it on a kneading board, and knead until smooth and elastic, put it back into the bowl, cover with a towel, and set aside overnight to rise. Next morning, lay the dough on a biscuit or kneading board again and knead well. Make into a loaf, put into a pan, and when well risen, moisten the top with a little cold water and bake in a moderate oven.

ZWIEBEL PLATZ

Take a piece of rye bread dough. After it has risen sufficiently roll out quite thin, butter a long cake pan and put in the rolled dough.
Brush with melted butter; chop some onions very fine, strew thickly on top of cake, sprinkle with salt, put flakes of butter here and there.
Another way is to chop up parsley and use in place of onions. Then called "Petersilien Platz."

VARIETY BREAD

Dissolve one cake of compressed yeast in two cups of lukewarm water or milk, add two teaspoons of salt, three cups of bread or wheat flour, one cup of cornmeal, one cup of rye flour and one-half cup of dark molasses, and mix very thoroughly. Let rise, shape into loaves, let rise again and bake in a moderate oven for forty-five minutes.

ROLLS

Take bread dough, when ready to shape into loaves and make a long even roll. Cut into small even pieces, and shape with thumb and fingers into round balls. Set close together in a shallow pan, let rise until double the bulk, and bake in a hot oven from ten to twenty minutes. If crusty rolls are desired, set apart in a shallow pan, bake well, and cool in draft.

TEA ROLLS

Scald one cup of milk and when lukewarm dissolve one cake of compressed yeast and add one and one-half cups of flour. Beat thoroughly, cover and allow to stand until light. Add one-quarter cup of sugar, one and one-half teaspoons of salt, two eggs, one-third cup of butter and enough flour to knead. Allow to rise again until light. Shape into round or small oblong finger rolls, and place in buttered pans close together, when light bake in hot oven.

CRESCENT ROLLS

Take bread or kitchen dough, and when well risen, toss on floured baking board, roll into a square sheet, one-quarter inch thick. Spread with melted butter, and cut into six-inch squares, then cut each square into two equal parts through opposite corners, thus forming two triangles.
Roll over and over from the longest side to the opposite corner and then shape the rolls into half moons or crescents. Place in floured or greased pans, rather far apart; brush with beaten yolk to which a little cold water has been added and sprinkle tops of crescents or horns with poppy seed. Set in warm place to and, when double its bulk, bake in hot oven until brown and crusty.

BUNS

Make same as tea rolls. When well risen mold into small round buns; place in well-greased pans, one inch apart. Coyer set aside to rise until light-- about one hour. Brush with egg diluted with water; bake twenty minutes, just before removing from the oven, brush with sugar moistened with a little water.

RAISIN OR CURRANT BUNS

Boil two large potatoes and strain the water into a pitcher, dissolve two-thirds cake of yeast in a cup. Put potatoes in a pan with a cup of sugar; large lump of butter, and teaspoon of salt. The heat of potatoes will melt the sugar and butter. Mash with large masher to a cream; pour in rest of potato water, add pint of flour and mix together. Then cover and set in a warm place all night. In the morning add more flour, mix quickly and put currants or raisins in as you turn the dough. This will keep them from settling in the bottom of the bread. Put in hot pans and bake in a hot oven. This makes a delicious holiday bread. Eat with butter, hot or cold.

BREAD STICKS

Take pieces of raised bread dough, roll three-eighths inch thick and four or five inches long. Place in floured pan, far apart, brush tops with beaten yolk and poppy seed. Let rise, bake in a hot oven until brown.

FRENCH ROLLS

Prepare the yeast as for bread and work just the same; add one-quarter cup of butter, one-quarter cup of sugar, one whole egg and one egg yolk beaten very light, flavor with mace or a few gratings of lemon peel; work until it leaves the hand perfectly clean, then form into rolls, let raise, brush with beaten egg, place rolls in pan close together and bake.

BUTTERED TOAST

Slice even slices of baker's bread, not too thin, put in biscuit pan on the top rack of a very hot oven, brown nicely on one side, then turn and brown on the other, spread with butter, and a little powdered sugar, if desired, and serve at once. Or put the slices on a long fork, hold before a red coal fire, without flame, toast on both sides and proceed as above.

MILK OR CREAM TOAST

Toast as many slices of stale light bread as desired a light brown. Heat milk or cream, allowing one-half cup for each slice, add small lump of butter. When just at the boiling point, pour over bread which has been placed in dish, sprinkle with sugar and cinnamon, cover, and serve immediately. Nice for invalids.

CINNAMON TOAST FOR TEA

Bread cut thin and browned, but not dried.

Butter the toast while very hot, thinly and evenly, and sprinkle over each piece some powdered cinnamon and sugar.

ARME RITTER

Beat two eggs slightly, add one-half teaspoon of salt and two-thirds cup of milk; dip six slices of stale bread in the mixture. Have a griddle hot and well buttered; brown the bread on each side. Serve hot with cinnamon and sugar or a sauce.

COFFEE CAKES (KUCHEN)

RENDERED BUTTER

Procure as much country or Western butter as desired, you may get several pounds of it when it is cheap during the summer; or any butter unfit for table use may be made sweet and good for cooking purposes and will last for months, if prepared in the following manner: Place the butter in a deep, iron kettle, filling only half full to prevent boiling over. Set it on the fire where it will simmer slowly for several hours.
Watch carefully that it does not boil over. Do not stir it, but from time to time skim it. When perfectly clear, and all the salt and sediment has settled at the bottom, the butter is done. Set aside a few minutes, then strain into stone jars through a fine sieve, and when cold tie up tightly with paper and cloth. Keep in a cool, dry place.

COFFEE CAKE (KUCHEN) DOUGH

Soak one-half ounce of yeast in one-half cup of lukewarm milk; when dissolved put in a bowl, or round agate pan, and stir in one cup of sifted flour, one teaspoon of sugar and one-fourth teaspoon of salt, mix thoroughly, and put in a warm place (not hot) to rise, from one to two hours.

When well risen, cream well together one cup of sugar and three-fourths cup of butter, then add three eggs, five cups of sifted flour, one cup of milk and one teaspoon of salt, mix together until light, then stir in the risen yeast, and with a spoon work well for ten minutes, and set aside to rise again, five or six hours or all night. Dough should not be very stiff. When well risen it can be used for cinnamon cake, pies or pocket books. This recipe makes one large cinnamon cake, three pies, and about one dozen pocket books. If set at night use half the quantity of yeast.

KAFFEE KUCHEN (CINNAMON)

Butter long and broad cake-pans thoroughly, roll out enough dough to cover them, and let it rise about half an hour before baking, then brush it well with melted butter. Sprinkle sugar and cinnamon on top and some chopped almonds. Take a small lump of butter, a very little flour, some sugar and cinnamon and rub it between the hands until it is like lumps of almonds, then strew on top of cakes.

CINNAMON ROLLS OR SCHNECKEN

Take half the kitchen dough. Roll one-half inch thick and spread well with melted butter. Sprinkle generously with scraped maple, brown or granulated sugar and cinnamon, then roll. Cut the roll into equal parts about one inch thick, place close together endwise in a spider, generously buttered, spread with one-fourth inch layer of brown, or maple sugar. Let rise until light, and bake ten to twenty minutes in a hot oven, a golden brown. Invert the spider, remove rolls and serve caramel side up.

ABGERUEHRTER KUGELHOPF

Soak one-half ounce of yeast or one cake compressed yeast in a very little lukewarm milk; add a pinch of salt and one tablespoon of sugar, stir it up smooth and set back of the stove to rise. In the meantime rub a scant cup of butter and a scant cup of powdered sugar to a cream, add gradually the yolks of four eggs, one at a time and add also the grated peel of a lemon. Sift two cups of flour into a bowl, make a depression in the centre, pour in, the yeast, one cup of lukewarm milk, and make a light batter of this. Add the creamed butter and eggs and stir until it forms blisters and leaves the bowl clean. Take one-half cup of cleaned and seeded dark raisins and cut up some citron very fine. Dredge flour over them before adding, and if necessary, add more flour to the dough, which should be of the consistency of cup cake batter. Last add the stiffly-beaten whites of the eggs. Place in a well-greased long or round pan with tube in centre; let rise until double in bulk, and bake in moderate oven until browned and thoroughly done.

PLAIN BUNT OR NAPF KUCHEN

Take one cake compressed yeast, add a pinch of salt, one tablespoon of sugar, and about two tablespoons of lukewarm water. Stir the yeast until it is a smooth paste and set it in a warm place to rise. Sift two and one-half cups of flour (use the same size cup for measuring everything you are going to use in your cake), make a depression in the centre, stir in the yeast and a scant cup of lukewarm milk, make batter, and let it rise until you have prepared the following: Rub one-half cup of butter and three-fourths cup of powdered sugar to a cream, just as for cup cake, then add gradually one egg at a time, using three altogether, and stirring all the time in one direction. Work in the risen batter two or three spoons at a time between each egg. Grate in the peel of a lemon or an orange. Butter the bunt-form well (do this always before you begin to work). Blanched almonds may be set in the grooves of the cake-form after buttering it. Put in the dough, set it in a warm place and let it rise for an hour and a half or two hours. Bake in a moderate oven one full hour, covered at first.

CHOCOLATE COFFEE CAKE

Pour a bunt kitchen dough into long, well-buttered tins, and when baked remove from the oven and cover thickly with boiled chocolate icing.

POCKET BOOKS

Take as much of the coffee cake dough as you desire, lay it on a well-floured biscuit board and mix just enough more flour with it to enable you to roll it out without sticking to the board. Roll out about one-fourth inch thick and cut the dough in squares about as long as your finger.

Beat the yolk of one egg and two tablespoons of milk together; wet each square well with the mixture, lay one raisin in the centre (after the seed has been removed from it), sprinkle thickly with sugar and cinnamon mixed together, then put a small dab of butter on top. Catch the four corners of each square together, so that the inside is protected. Lay the pocket books, not too closely together, in a greased pan and set aside to rise. When well risen bake in a moderately hot oven until well baked and browned nicely.

BOLA

Make a good, rich bread dough. Let it rise overnight; next morning; mix with dough two eggs; one-half pound of butter well kneaded; stand by fire until well risen. When risen, roll out into thin sheets and sprinkle with chopped almonds, citron, cinnamon and plenty of brown sugar and lumps of butter all through; roll up like jelly-roll, cut in pieces a finger long, grease pan, stand pieces in centre, others around and let rise before baking. Watch it well while baking.

FRENCH COFFEE CAKE (SAVARIN)

Soak one cake of compressed yeast in a little lukewarm water or milk.
Put the yeast in a cup, add two tablespoons of lukewarm water, a pinch of salt and one tablespoon of sugar, stir it up well with a spoon and set back of the stove to rise. Rub one-half cup of butter to a cream, add one-third cup of powdered sugar and stir constantly in one direction. Add the yolks of four eggs, one at a time, and the grated peel of a lemon. Sift two cups of flour into a bowl, make a depression in the centre of the flour, pour in the yeast and one cup of lukewarm milk. Stir and make a light batter of this. Add the creamed butter and eggs, stir until it forms blisters and leaves the bowl clean; one-half cup of dark raisins, one-half cup of pounded almonds and a little citron, cut up very fine, and last the stiff-beaten whites of the eggs.
Fill your cake forms which have been well-greased, set in a warm place to rise until double in bulk, about forty-five minutes, and bake in a moderate oven forty-five minutes. Fill the centre with whipped cream and serve with rum sauce.

BABA A LA PARISIENNE

Prepare the yeast as above; cream a scant cup of butter with four tablespoons of sugar, the grated peel of a lemon, add five eggs, one at a time, stirring each egg a few minutes before you add the next. Have ready two cups of sifted flour and add two spoonfuls between each egg until all is used. Make a soft dough of the yeast, a scant cup of lukewarm milk, add two spoonfuls between each egg until all is used up, a pinch of salt, and one cup of flour. Let it rise for fifteen minutes.
Now mix all well, rub the form with butter, and blanch one-half cup of almonds, cut into long strips and strew all over the form. Fill in the mixture or cake batter, let it rise two hours and bake very slowly.

MOHN (POPPY SEED) ROLEY POLEY

Roll out a piece of dough large enough to cover your whole baking-board, roll thin. Let it rise until you have prepared the filling; grind one cup of black poppy seed in a coffee-mill as tight as possible and clean it well, throw away the first bit you grind so as not to have the coffee taste; put it on to boil with one cup of milk, add two tablespoons of butter, one-half cup of seeded raisins, one-half cup of walnuts or almonds chopped up fine, two tablespoons of molasses or syrup, and a little citron cut up fine. When thick, set it away to cool, and if not sweet enough add more sugar and flavor with vanilla. When this mixture has cooled, spread on the dough which has risen by this time. Take up one corner and roll it up, into a long roll, like a jelly-roll, put in a greased pan and let it rise an hour, then spread butter on top and bake very slowly. Let it get quite brown, so as to bake through thoroughly.

When cold cut up in slices, as many as you are going to use at one time only.

MOHN WACHTEL

Take coffee cake dough. Let the dough rise again; for an hour, spread with a poppy seed mixture, after cutting into squares, fold into triangles and pinch the edges together. Lay in well-buttered pans, about two inches apart, and let them rise again, spread with poppy seed filling. Take one-half pound of poppy seed (mohn) which have previously been soaked in milk and then ground, add one-quarter of a pound of sugar and the yolks of three eggs. Stir this all together in one direction until quite thick and then stir in the beaten whites to which you must add two ounces of sifted flour and one-quarter of a pound of melted butter. Fill the tartlets and bake. The poppy seed filling in Mohn Roley Poley may be used in the Mohn Wachtel if so desired.

MOHNTORTS

Line a deep pie-plate with a thin sheet of kuchen dough, let it rise about half an hour, then fill with a poppy seed filling same as used with Mohn Wachtel. Fill the pie-plates and bake.

SMALL MOHN CAKES

Roll coffee cake dough out quite thin, spread with melted butter (a brush is best for this purpose). Let it rise a little while, then sprinkle well with one cup of sugar, add one-half pound of ground poppy seed moistened with one-half cup of water, cut into strips about an inch wide and four-inches long; roll and put in a well-buttered pan to rise, leaving enough space between each and brush, with butter. Bake in moderate oven at first, then increase the heat; bake slowly.

BERLINER PFANNKUCHEN (PURIM KRAPFEN)

Take one and one-half cups of flour, a pinch of salt sifted into a deep bowl, one cup of lukewarm milk and three-fourths cake of compressed yeast which has been, dissolved in a little warm water and sugar. Stir into a dough, cover with a towel and set away in a warm place to rise.
When well risen, take one-half cup of butter, one cup of sugar, a little salt and rub to a cream. Add two eggs well beaten, stir all well and add the risen dough, one teaspoon of salt and work in gradually five cups of sifted flour and the grated peel of a lemon. Stir the dough till it blisters and leaves the dish perfectly clean at the sides. Let the dough rise slowly for about two hours (all yeast dough is better if it rises slowly). Take a large baking-board, flour well and roll out the dough on it as thin as a double thickness of pasteboard. When it is all rolled out, cut with a round cutter the size of a tumbler. When all the dough has been cut out, beat up an egg. Spread the beaten egg; on the edge of each cake (spread only a few at a time for they would get too dry if all were done at once). Then put one-half teaspoon of marmalade, jam or jelly on the cake. Put another cake on top of one already spread, having cut it with a cutter a little bit smaller than the one used in the first place. This makes them stick better and prevents the preserves coming out while cooking. Set all away on a floured board or pan about two inches apart. Spread the top of each cake with melted butter and let them rise from one to two hours. When ready to fry, heat at least two pounds of rendered butter or any good vegetable oil in a deep iron kettle. Try the butter with a small piece of dough. If it rises immediately, put in the doughnuts. In putting them in, place the side that is up on the board down in the hot butter. Do not crowd them in the kettle as they require room to rise and spread. Cover them with a lid.

In a few seconds uncover. If they are light brown, turn them over on the other side but do not cover them again. When done they will have a white stripe around the centre. Take them up with a perforated skimmer, lay on a large platter, sprinkle with pulverized sugar. If the butter gets too hot take from the fire a minute. These are best eaten fresh.

The doughnuts may be baked in moderately hot oven and when half done glazed with sugar and white of egg.

TOPFA DALKELN. CHEESE CAKES (HUNGARIAN)

Take one-half ounce of yeast, mix with a little scalded milk which has cooled to lukewarm, one-half cup of flour and put aside in a warm place to rise. Allow two cups of scalded milk to become lukewarm. Add one pound of flour (four cups sifted flour) to the risen sponge, then the two cups of milk, mix these very well, cover with a cloth and put aside in a warm place to rise. Take one pound of sweet pot cheese, a pinch of salt, three egg yolks, rind of one lemon, one-half cup of light colored raisins and sugar to taste; mix very well and add the beaten whites and mix thoroughly. When the dough is very well risen, place on a pastry board, roll out and spread with melted butter, fold these edges over to the middle, then the top and bottom over, roll again and spread with butter, fold all sides in once more, roll, spread with butter, repeat the folding, roll out to one-half inch thickness, cut in three-inch squares, place a tablespoon of the cheese mixture in the centre of each square, fold over opposite corners, spread egg white over the top of each pocket, let rise fifteen minutes or one-half hour and bake in a hot oven; when they are well risen, lower heat and bake to a golden brown.
This will make about thirty cakes. The dough in the above may be used with the following filling:

Boil and stone one-half pound of prunes, mash to a pulp, sweeten, add the grated peel of a lemon, some cinnamon, etc., and put one teaspoon of this into each square. Take up the corners, fasten them firmly, also pinch all along the edges and lay in a buttered pan, let them rise half an hour before baking. Spread them with melted butter, and bake a nice brown.

PUFFS (PURIM)

Make the dough same as for Berliner Pfannkuchen, and when well risen roll out on a floured board one-half inch thick, cut in triangles, lay on floured dishes or board to rise. When well risen, drop into a deep kettle of boiling butter and with a spoon baste with the butter until brown; remove with a perforated skimmer and sprinkle with powdered sugar.

KINDLECH

Into a large bowl sift one pound of fine flour. Make a depression in the centre and pour into it one yeast cake dissolved in a little milk. Let this remain until the milk and yeast have risen a little. Stir in the surrounding flour together with three well-beaten eggs, a quarter of a pound of butter, six ounces of sugar, a pinch of salt and two cups of lukewarm milk. Knead the whole into a smooth dough.

Roll this out very lightly on a well-floured board, brush over with a feather dipped in melted butter and strew thickly with chopped almonds, sultanas and currants. Next fold over about three fingers' width of the dough. Brush the upper surface of this fold with melted butter and strew with mixed fruit and almonds. Fold over again and repeat the operation until the whole of the dough is folded up in layer somewhat resembling a flattened, roley poley pudding. Brush the top well with another feather dipped in beaten egg and cut the whole into thick slices or fingers. Let them stand for half an hour and then bake for an hour in a rather slow oven.

A CHEAP COFFEE CAKE

This German coffee cake is made by kneading into a pint of bread dough one well-beaten egg, one-half cup of sugar, and a generous tablespoon of butter. The mixture is rolled flat, placed in a shallow pan, let rise again until very light, sprinkled with finely chopped nuts, dusted over with sugar and cinnamon and baked in a quick oven.

BOHEMIAN KOLATCHEN

Make kuchen dough. Add a little cinnamon and mace and one teaspoon of anise seed, well pounded, or flavor to taste. Let rise till very light, then take out on mixing board and roll out to about one-half inch in thickness. Cut in rounds three inches in diameter and lay on a well-buttered pan, pressing down the centre of each so as to raise a ridge around the edge. When well risen, brush the top over with stiffly-beaten white of an egg and sprinkle with granulated sugar.

ZWIEBACK

Scald one-half cup of milk and when lukewarm add to one cake of compressed yeast. Add one-fourth cup of sugar, one-fourth cup of melted butter, one-half teaspoon of salt and three eggs unbeaten, one-half teaspoon of powdered anise and enough flour to handle. Let rise until light. Make into oblong rolls the length of middle finger and place together in a buttered pan in parallel rows, two inches apart. Let rise again and bake twenty minutes. When cold, cut in one-half inch slices and brown evenly in the oven.

SOUR CREAM KOLATCHEN

Cream one-half cup of butter, add five yolks, two tablespoons of sugar, grated rind of a lemon, one cup of thick sour cream and one ounce or two cakes of yeast dissolved with a little sugar in two tablespoons of lukewarm milk. Stir all together and add three cups of flour; mix and drop from end of teaspoon on well-greased pans. Let rise until light in a warm place. Place a raisin or cherry on the top of each cake, spread with beaten white of egg, sprinkle with sugar and bake ten minutes in a hot oven.

RUSSIAN TEA CAKES

Mix one cup of sugar, one cup of eggs (about five), and one cup of sour cream with enough flour to roll. Toss on board, roll out one-fourth inch thick, spread with a thin layer of butter, fold the dough over, roll and spread again; repeat three or four times, using altogether three-fourths pound of brick butter. Then place dough in a bowl, cover, and let stand on ice to harden. Then roll as thin as possible, strew with one cup of chopped almonds, sugar and cinnamon, and cut into seven-inch strips.
Roll each strip separately into a roll, cut into squares and strew top with chopped almonds, sugar and cinnamon. Bake in a hot oven.

WIENER KIPFEL

Dissolve one ounce of yeast in one-half cup of lukewarm milk, a pinch of salt and one tablespoon of sugar, set away in a warm place to rise. Sift one pound of flour into a deep bowl and make a dough of one cup of lukewarm milk and the yeast. Set it away until you have prepared the following: Rub a quarter of a pound of butter and four ounces of sugar to a cream, adding yolks of three eggs and one whole egg. Add this to the dough and work well. Let it rise about one hour, then roll out on a well-floured board, just as you would for cookies and let it rise again for at least one-half hour. Spread with beaten whites of eggs, raisins, almonds and citron. Cut dough into triangles. Pinch the edges together.
Lay them in well-buttered pans about two inches apart and let then rise again. Then spread again with stiff-beaten whites of eggs and lay a few pounded almonds on each one. Bake a light yellow.

SPICE ROLL

Roll out coffee cake dough quite thin and let it rise half an hour, brush with melted butter and make a filling of the following: Grate some lebkuchen or plain gingerbread; add one-half cup of almonds or nuts, one cup of seeded raisins and one cup of cleaned currants. Strew these all over the dough together with some brown sugar and a little syrup. Spice with cinnamon and roll. Spread with butter and let it rise for an hour.
Bake brown.

WIENER STUDENTEN KIPFEL

Make dough same as for Wiener Kipfel. Roll it out quite thin on a well-floured board and let it rise. Cut also into triangles (before you cut them, spread with melted butter). Mix one cup of chopped fresh walnuts with one cup of brown sugar, juice of a lemon, or grind the nuts; add cream to make a paste, sugar to taste and flavor with vanilla, and fill the triangles with the mixture. Take up the three corners and pinch together tightly. Set in well-buttered pans and let them rise again and spread or brush each one with melted butter. Bake a light brown.

YEAST KRANTZ

Take coffee cake dough, add one-fourth cup of washed currants. Let rise in warm place, then toss on floured board. Divide into three or four equal parts, roll each part into a long strand and work the strands together to form one large braid. Place braid in form of a circle in greased baking-pan or twist the braid to resemble the figure eight, pretzel shape. Let rise again in a warm place and bake in a moderate oven one-half hour or until thoroughly done. Brush with beaten eggs and sugar, sprinkle with a few chopped almonds. Return to oven to brown slightly.

STOLLEN

Sift two pounds of flour into a bowl and set a sponge in it with one cake of compressed yeast, one teaspoon of salt, one pint of lukewarm milk and one tablespoon of sugar. When this has risen, add one-half pound of creamed butter, a quarter of a pound of seeded raisins and one-quarter of a pound of sugar, yolks of four eggs, four ounces of powdered almonds, and the grated peel of a lemon. Work all well, beating with the hands, not kneading. Let this dough rise at least three hours, roll, press down the centre and fold over double, then form into one or two long loaves, narrow at the end. Brush the top with melted butter, let rise again and bake three-quarters of an hour in a moderate oven.

APPLE CAKE (KUCHEN)

After the pan is greased with butter, roll out a piece of dough quite thin, lay it in the pan, press a rim out of the dough all around the pan and let it rise for about ten minutes. Pare five large apples, core and quarter them, dipping each piece in melted butter before laying on the cake, sprinkle bountifully with sugar (brown being preferable to white for this purpose) and cinnamon. See that you have tart apples. Leave the cake in the pans and cut out the pieces just as you would want to serve them. If they stick to the pan, set the pan on top of the hot stove for a minute and the cake will then come out.

CHEESE CAKE OR PIE

Take one and one-half cups of cheese, rub smooth with a silver or wooden spoon through a colander or sieve, then rub a piece of sweet butter the size of an egg to a cream, add gradually one-half cup of sugar and the yolks of three eggs, a pinch of salt, grate in the peel of a lemon, one-half cup of cleaned currants and a little citron cut up very fine.

Line two pie-plates with some kuchen dough or pie dough (See "Coffee Cakes (Kuchen)"), roll it out quite thin, butter the pie-plates quite heavily, and let the dough in them rise at least a quarter of an hour before putting in the cheese mixture, for it must be baked immediately after the cheese is put in, and just before you put the cheese into the plates whip up the whites of the eggs to a very stiff froth and stir through the cheese mixture.

CHERRY CAKE

Line a cake-pan, which has been well-buttered, with a thin layer of kuchen dough. Stone two pounds of cherries and lay them on a sieve with a dish underneath to catch the juice. Sprinkle sugar over them and bake.

In the meantime beat up four eggs with a cup of sugar, beat until light and add the cherry juice. Draw the kuchen to the oven door, pour this mixture over it and bake.

PEACH KUCHEN

Grease your cake-pans thoroughly with good clarified butter, then line them with a rich coffee cake dough which has been rolled very thin and set in a warm place to rise. Then pare and quarter enough peaches to cover the dough. Lay the peaches in rows and sweeten and set in oven to bake. Make a meringue quickly as possible and pour over the cakes and bake a light brown.

FRESH PRUNE CAKE (KUCHEN)

Line a greased biscuit-pan with some of the coffee cake dough. Roll the dough thin and let it come up on the sides of the pan, then set aside to rise. When risen, cut the prunes in halves (they must be the fresh ones, not dried), lay in rows thickly and close together all over the bottom of the pan, do not leave any space between the prunes. Sprinkle very thickly with sugar, lightly with cinnamon, and lay bits of fresh butter all over the top. Bake until done in a moderately hot oven.

PRUNE CAKE (KUCHEN)

Line one or two plates with a thin roll of kuchen dough and let it rise again in the pans which have been heavily greased. Have some prunes boiled very soft, take out the kernels, mash them until like mush, sweeten to taste, add cinnamon and grated peel of a lemon or lemon juice, put in the lined pie-plates and bake immediately. Serve with whipped cream, sweetened and flavored.

HUCKLEBERRY KUCHEN

Line your cake-pans, which should be long and narrow, with a rich kuchen dough, having previously greased them well. Make a paste of cornstarch, one cup of milk, one tablespoon of butter and one teaspoon of cornstarch wet with cold milk. Boil until thick, sweeten and flavor with vanilla and spread on top of the cake dough, then sprinkle thickly with huckleberries which have been carefully picked, sugared and sprinkled with ground cinnamon. Bake in a quick oven.

HUCKLEBERRY PIE

Clean, pick and wash two cups of huckleberries, then drain them. Beat yolk of one egg and two tablespoons of sugar until light, add one tablespoon of milk, then the drained berries. Line one pie-plate with rich pastry or cookie dough, pour on it the berry mixture, put in the oven and bake light brown; remove from the oven, spread with a meringue made of the white of the egg beaten stiff, and two tablespoons of sugar added. Brown nicely. The white can be beaten with the yolk and sugar, if preferred.

MUFFINS AND BISCUITS

BAKING-POWDER

Put eight ounces of bicarbonate of soda, one ounce of tartaric acid and one package of high-grade cornstarch together and sift them thoroughly five times. Keep closely covered in glass jars or tin boxes.

BAKING-POWDER BATTERS

Batter is a mixture of flour with sufficient liquid to make it thin enough to be beaten.

Pour-batter requires one measure of liquid to one measure of flour.

Drop-batter requires one measure of liquid to two measures of flour.

To make a batter. Sift flour before measuring. Put flour by spoonfuls into the cup; do not press or shake down. Mix and sift dry ingredients.
Measure dry, then liquid ingredients, shortening may be rubbed or chopped in while cold, or creamed; or it may be melted and then added to dry ingredients, or added after the liquid. Use two teaspoons of baking-powder to one cup of flour. If eggs are used, less baking-powder will be required.

When sour milk is used, take one level teaspoon of soda to a pint of milk; when molasses is used, take one teaspoon of soda or baking-powder to each cup of molasses.

Mix dry materials in one bowl and liquids in another, combine them quickly, handle as little as possible and put at once into the oven.

The oven for baking biscuits should be hot enough to brown a teaspoon of flour in one minute.

BROWN BREAD

Mix and sift together one cup each of rye, graham flour, corn-meal and one teaspoon of salt. Dissolve one teaspoon of soda in one cup of molasses. Add alternately to flour with two cups of sour milk. Grease one-pound baking-powder cans, put in the dough and boil two and one-half hours, keeping the water always three-fourths up around the tins. Turn out on baking-tins and place in the oven fifteen minutes to brown.

To be eaten warm, whatever is left over can be steamed again or toasted.

CORN BREAD

Mix and sift one cup of corn-meal, one cup of flour, two tablespoons of sugar, one-half teaspoon of salt, three teaspoons of baking-powder. Melt one tablespoon of butter and add to one egg; mix milk and egg and beat this into the dry ingredients, pour this mixture into well-greased tins and bake in a hot oven one-half hour. Cut in squares and serve hot. Bake in gem tins if preferred.

BRAN BREAD

Sift four teaspoons of soda, two teaspoons of salt with four cups of white flour, add four cups of bran flour and mix well. Add one cup of molasses and four cups of sweet milk. Use chopped nuts or raisins or both as desired. This will make three or four flat loaves. Place in greased pans (four and a half by nine inches), and bake one hour in a moderate oven.

JOHNNIE CAKE

Mix one cup flour and two cups corn-meal, one heaping teaspoon of soda, one-half cup sugar, add two eggs beaten with one and one-half cups of buttermilk, one half cup of molasses and one-half cup of shortening, melted. Beat all ingredients as fast as possible for a minute. Pour the dough into a warm, well-buttered pan and bake quickly and steadily for half an hour. The dough should be as soft as gingerbread dough. Serve hot.

EGGLESS GINGERBREAD WITH CHEESE

Sift two cups of flour, one teaspoon of soda, one-half teaspoon of salt and two teaspoons of ginger. Melt three-fourths cup of grated cheese in one-half cup of hot water, add one-half cup of molasses and blend perfectly. Add the flour and seasonings very gradually and beat thoroughly. Bake in muffin rings for fifteen minutes and serve while warm.

GINGERBREAD

To one cup of molasses add one cup of milk, sour or sweet, dissolve one teaspoon of soda in the milk, one tablespoon of butter, one or two eggs, one teaspoon of ginger and one of ground cinnamon, add enough sifted flour to make a light batter. Bake in a shallow pan.

WHITE NUT BREAD

Mix two and one-half cups of flour, four teaspoons of baking-powder, one-half teaspoon of salt, one-half cup of sugar and one-half cup of walnut meats, broken; add one egg beaten with one cup of milk and let this mixture stand for about twenty minutes in well-greased breadpan before placing in a moderate oven to bake. Bake about an hour. Better day after it is made.

BAKING-POWDER BISCUITS

Sift two cups of flour with one-half teaspoon of salt, four teaspoons of baking-powder, and four tablespoons of butter; cut butter in with two knives and mix with one-half to two-thirds cup of water or milk, stir this in quickly with a knife, when well mixed place on a well-floured board and roll out about one inch thick, work quickly, cut with a biscuit cutter or the cover of a half-pound baking-powder can; place on a greased pan and bake quickly in a well-heated quick oven tea to fifteen minutes.

Butter substitutes may be used in place of butter.

DROP BISCUIT

Add to ingredients for baking-powder biscuit enough more milk or water to make a thick drop batter, about two tablespoons; mix as directed for biscuit, drop by spoonfuls an inch apart on a greased baking-sheet or into greased gem pans, small size.

The more crust the more palatable these biscuits are. The mixture should not be soft enough to run. Bake in a hot oven ten to twelve minutes.

SOUR MILK BISCUITS

Mix and sift two cups of flour, one-half teaspoon of salt and one-half

COVERED CHEESE CAKE

Cream one cup of sugar with butter the size of an egg, add two eggs well beaten and one cup of water alternately with two and one-half cups of flour in which has been sifted two teaspoons of baking-powder.

Filling.--Beat two eggs with one-half cup of sugar, add one-half pound of pot cheese, one tablespoon of cornstarch boiled in one cup of milk, cool this and add, flavor with lemon extract.

Put one-half of the batter in cake pan, then the filling and the other half of batter. Bake in slow oven thirty-five minutes. Sift sugar on top when done.

BLITZ KUCHEN

Take one cup of powdered sugar, one-half cup of butter, one cup of pastry flour, one-quarter of a teaspoon of baking-powder, peel and juice of one lemon, five or six eggs. Beat sugar with two whole eggs; add butter, beat until foamy; after that the flour mixed with baking-powder, lemon and four yolks. Last the stiffly-beaten whites of the eggs. Mix this well, bake in form in a moderately hot oven.

KOENIG KUCHEN

Cream one-quarter cup of butter with one cup of sugar, yolks of six eggs, one-quarter pound of raisins, one-quarter pound of currants, juice and peel of one lemon, one spoon of rum, twenty blanched and grated almonds, two cups of flour mixed with one-half teaspoon of baking-powder, two stiffly-beaten whites of eggs. Bake in an ungreased form one to one and one-half hours.

NUT CAKE

Take one-half cup of butter, three eggs, one and one-half cups of sugar, two and one-half cups of flour, two and one-half level teaspoons of baking-powder, and one-half cup of milk. One cup of any kind of nuts.

Rub the butter and sugar to a light white cream; add the eggs beaten a little; then the flour sifted with the powder. Mix with the milk and nuts into a rather firm batter. Bake in a paper lined tin in a steady oven thirty-five minutes.

LOAF COCOANUT CAKE

Rub one cup of butter and two cups of sugar to a cream. Add one cup of milk, whites of four eggs, three cups of flour (measure after sifting), and three teaspoons of baking-powder added in last sifting. Add a grated cocoanut and last the stiffly-beaten whites. Bake in a loaf. Line tin with buttered paper.

FRUIT CAKE (WEDDING CAKE)

Take one pound of butter and one pound of sugar rubbed to a cream, yolks of twelve eggs, one tablespoon of cinnamon, one teaspoon of allspice, one-half teaspoon of mace, one-half teaspoon of cloves, one-fourth of a pound of almonds pounded, two pounds of raisins (seeded and chopped), three pounds of currants (carefully cleaned), one pound of citron (shredded very fine), and one-quarter of a pound of orange peel (chopped very fine). Soak all this prepared fruit in one pint of brandy overnight. Add all to the dough and put in the stiffly-beaten whites last. Bake in a very slow oven for several hours, in cake pans lined with buttered paper. When cold wrap in cloths dipped in brandy and put in earthen jars. If baked in gas oven have light very low. Keep oven the same temperature for four or five hours.

APPLE SAUCE CAKE

This apple sauce cake will be found as delicious and tasty as the rich fruit cake, which is so difficult to prepare, and it is very much less expensive.

In a big mixing bowl, beat to a creamy consistency four tablespoons of butter, one egg and one cup of sugar. Add a saltspoon of salt, one teaspoon of allspice, one teaspoon of vanilla and a little grated nutmeg. Beat and stir all these ingredients well together with the other mixture, then add one cup of chopped raisins, after dusting them with flour. Mix these well through the dough and then add one cup of unsweetened apple sauce which has been pressed through a fine wire sieve. After this is well mixed with the other ingredients, stir in one teaspoon of baking-soda dissolved in one tablespoon of boiling water.

Last of all, stir in one cup of flour, sifting twice after measuring it.

Bake forty-five minutes in moderate oven.

The tendency in making this cake is to get the dough too thin, therefore the apple sauce should be cooked quite thick, and then if the dough is still too thin add more flour. Bake one hour in moderate oven. This cake can be made with chicken schmalz in place of butter. Ice with plain white frosting.

SPICE CAKE

This spice cake is economical, easy to make and delicious, three qualities which must appeal to the housewife.

Cream one cup of brown sugar and one-half cup of butter (or a little less of any butter substitute). Add one-half teaspoon of ground cloves and ground cinnamon, one cup of sour milk; one teaspoon of baking-soda, two cups of flour and one cup of raisins chopped. Have ready a warm oven and bake three-quarters of an hour.

GREEN TREE LAYER CAKE AND ICING

One cup of granulated sugar, one-half cup of butter, three eggs, one cup of milk, two and one-half scant cups of sifted flour, one teaspoon of vanilla extract, two teaspoons of baking-powder. Cream the butter and sugar together as usual, and then break in three eggs and beat until very creamy. Add the flour and milk alternately, reserving a little of the flour to add after the vanilla and baking-powder. Beat well and bake in layer cake tins. The entire success and lightness of this cake depends upon the beating of the sugar, butter and eggs. If these are beaten long enough they will become as creamy and fluffy as whipped cream.

Icing for This Cake.--One and one-half cups of confectioner's sugar (not powdered), butter the size of a large egg, two tablespoons of cocoa, one teaspoon of vanilla, moisten to make the mixture the consistence of very thick cream. Cream or whipped cream may be used for the mixing, but many like this icing when made with lukewarm coffee. The sugar and butter are creamed together thoroughly and then the cocoa and vanilla are added, and lastly the cream or coffee. This is a good imitation of German tree cake. The icing on tree cake is an inch thick, and it is marked to represent the bark of a tree. The way it is served is with a little green candy on it, and it is really very delicious although extremely rich. The thicker or rather firmer this icing is, the better.

EGGLESS, BUTTERLESS, MILKLESS CAKE

One package of seeded raisins, two cups of sugar, two cups of boiling water, one teaspoon of cinnamon, one teaspoon of cloves, two tablespoons of Crisco, chicken schmalz or clarified drippings, one-half teaspoon of salt. Boil all together five minutes, cool, add one teaspoon of soda dissolved in water, three cups of flour. Bake forty-five minutes, make two cakes in layer pans.

APPLE JELLY CAKE

Rub one cup of butter and two cups of sugar to a cream, add four eggs, whites beaten separately, one cup of milk, two teaspoons of baking-powder and three and one-half cups of flour. Bake in layer tins.

Filling.--Pare and grate three large apples ("Greenings" preferred), the juice and peel of a lemon, one cup of sugar and one well-beaten egg.
Put in ingredients together and boil, stirring constantly until thick.
Cool and fill in cake.

CREAM LAYER CAKE

Rub one cup of butter and two scant cups of sugar to a cream; the yolks of four eggs beaten in well, add gradually one cup of milk and three cups of sifted flour, and add three teaspoons of baking-powder in last sifting; put whites in last. Bake in layers as for jelly cake. When cold, spread with the following filling: Moisten two tablespoons of cornstarch with enough cold milk to work it into a paste. Scald one-half pint of milk with one-half cup of sugar and a pinch of salt. Beat the yolks of two eggs light; add the cornstarch to this, and as soon as the milk is scalded pour in the mixture gradually, stirring constantly until thick. Drop in one teaspoon of sweet butter, and when this is mixed in, set away until cool. Spread between layers.

COCOANUT LAYER CAKE

Rub to a cream one-half cup of butter and one and one-half cups of pulverized sugar. Add gradually three eggs, one-half cup of milk and two cups of flour, adding two teaspoons of baking-powder in last sifting.
Bake in layers.

Filling.--One grated cocoanut and all of its milk, to half of which add the beaten whites of two eggs and one cup of powdered sugar. Lay this between the layers. Mix with the other half of the grated cocoanut five tablespoons of powdered sugar and strew thickly on top of cake, which has been previously iced.

CHOCOLATE LAYER CAKE

Stir one scant half cup of butter to a cream with one cup of sugar. Add alternately one-half cup of sweet milk, yolks of two eggs which you have previously beaten until quite light, add whites of two, and one-half cup of sifted flour. Make a custard of one-half cup of milk, with one cup of grated chocolate, one-half cup of granulated sugar; boil until thick, add the yolk of one egg, then remove from the fire; stir until cool, add this to the cake batter, add one and one-half cups of sifted flour, two teaspoons of baking-powder and one of vanilla flavoring. Bake in layers and ice between and on top with plain white icing flavored to taste. You may substitute almond or colored icing.

CARAMEL LAYER CAKE

Place one-half cup of sugar in pan over fire. Stir until liquid smokes and burns brown. Add one-half cup of boiling water and cook into syrup.
Take one cup butter, one and one-half cups of sugar, yolks of two eggs, over one cup of water and two cups of flour. Beat all thoroughly. Add enough of the burnt sugar to flavor, also one teaspoon of vanilla, another half cup of

flour, two teaspoons of baking-powder and whites of two eggs. Bake in two layers, using remainder of burnt sugar for icing.

HUCKLEBERRY CAKE

Stir to a cream one cup of butter and two cups of powdered sugar and add gradually the yolks of four eggs. Sift into this three cups of flour, adding two teaspoons of baking-powder in the last sifting and add one cup of sweet milk alternately with the flour to the creamed butter, sugar and yolks. Spice with one teaspoon of cinnamon and add the stiff-beaten whites of the eggs. Lastly, stir in two cups of huckleberries which have been carefully picked over and well dredged with flour. Be careful in stirring in the huckleberries that you do not bruise them. You will find a wooden spoon the best for this purpose, the edges not being so sharp. Bake in a moderately hot oven; try with a straw, if it comes out clean, your cake is baked. This will keep fresh for a long while.

CREAM PUFFS

One cup of hot water, one-half cup of butter; boil together, and while boiling stir in one cup of sifted flour dry; take from the stove and stir to a thin paste, and after this cools add three eggs unbeaten, and stir vigorously for five minutes. Drop in tablespoonfuls on a buttered tin and bake in a quick oven twenty-five minutes, opening the oven door no oftener than is absolutely necessary, and being careful that they do not touch each other in the pan. This amount will make twelve puffs.
Cream for puffs: one cup of milk, one cup of sugar, one egg, three tablespoons of flour, vanilla to flavor. Stir the flour in a little of the milk; boil the rest, turn this in and stir until the whole thickens.
When both this and the puffs are cool open the puff a little way with a sharp knife and fill them with the cream.

CHOCOLATE ECLAIRS

To make eclairs spread the batter, prepared as in foregoing recipe, in long ovals and when done cover with plain or chocolate frosting, as follows: Boil one cup of brown sugar with one-half cup of molasses, one tablespoon of butter and two tablespoons of flour. Boil for one-half hour, then stir in one-

fourth pound of grated chocolate wet in one-fourth cup of sweet milk and boil until it hardens on the spoon.
Flavor with vanilla. Spread this upon the eclairs.

DOBOS TORTE

Cream yolks of six eggs with one-half pound of powdered sugar; add three-fourths cup of flour sifted three times; then add beaten whites of six eggs lightly and carefully into the mixture. Butter pie plates on under side and sprinkle with flour lightly over the butter and spread the mixture very thin. This amount makes one cake of twelve layers.
Remove layers at once with a spatula.

Filling.--Cream one-half pound of sweet butter and put on ice immediately; take one-half pound of sweet chocolate and break it into a cup of strong liquid coffee; add one-half pound of granulated sugar and let it boil until you can pull it almost like candy; remove from fire and stir the chocolate until it is quite cold. When cold add the chocolate mixture to the creamed butter. This filling is spread thin between the layers, spread the icing thicker on top and sides of the cake. This is very fine, but care must be taken in baking and removing the layers, as layers are as thin as wafers. Bake and make filling a day or two before needed.

SPONGE CAKE

Weigh any number of eggs, take the same weight of sugar and one-half the weight of flour; the grated rind and juice of one lemon to five eggs.
For mixing this cake, see the directions given in "To Bake Cakes"; the mixture should be very light and spongy, great care being used not to break down the whipped whites. The oven should be moderate at first, and the heat increased after a time. The cake must not be moved or jarred while baking. The time will be forty to fifty minutes according to size of cake. Use powdered sugar for sponge-cake. Rose-water makes a good flavoring when a change from lemon is wanted.

SMALL SPONGE CAKES

Separate the whites and yolks of four eggs, beat the whites stiff, and beat into them one-half cup of granulated sugar. Beat the yolks to a very stiff froth and beat into them one-half cup of granulated sugar.

This last mixture must be beaten for exactly five minutes. Add the juice and grated rind of one small lemon; beat yolks and whites together well, then stir in very gently one scant cup of flour that has been sifted three times. Remember that every stroke of the spoon after the flour is added toughens the cake just that much, so fold the flour in just enough to mix well. If baked in small patty pans they taste just like lady fingers. Bake twenty or twenty-five minutes in moderate oven.

DOMINOES

Make a sponge cake batter, and bake in long tins, not too large. The batter should not exceed the depth of one-fourth of an inch, spread it evenly and bake it in a quick oven (line the tins with buttered paper).

As each cake is taken from the oven, turn it upside down on a clean board or paper. Spread with a thin layer of currant or cranberry jelly, and lay the other cake on top of it. With a hot, sharp knife cut into strips like dominoes; push them with the knife about an inch apart, and ice them with ordinary white icing, putting a tablespoonful on each piece, the heat of the cake will soften it, and with little assistance the edges and sides may be smoothly covered. Set the cakes in a warm place, where the frosting will dry. Make a horn of stiff white paper with just a small opening; at the lower end. Put in one spoon of dark chocolate icing and close the horn at the top, and by pressing out the icing from the small opening, draw a line of it across the centre of each cake, and then make dots like those on dominoes. Keep the horn supplied with the icing.

LADY FINGERS

Beat the yolks of three eggs until light and creamy, add one-quarter pound of powdered sugar (sifted) and continue beating; add flavoring to taste, vanilla, lemon juice, grated rind of lemon or orange. To the whites of the three eggs add one-half saltspoon of salt and beat until very stiff. Stir in lightly one-half cup of flour and then fold in the beaten whites very gently. Press the mixture through a pastry tube on a baking-tin, covered with paper in portions one-half inch wide by four inches long, or drop on oblong molds; sift a little powdered sugar on top of each cake, and bake from ten to fifteen minutes in a moderate oven. Do not let brown. Remove immediately from pan, brush the flat surface of one cake with white of egg and press the underside of a second cake upon the first.

JELLY ROLL

Take three eggs creamed with one cup of granulated sugar, one cup of flour sifted with two teaspoons of baking-powder, add one-half cup of boiling water. Bake in broad pan--while hot, remove from pan and lay on cloth wet with cold water. Spread with jelly and roll quickly. Sprinkle with powdered sugar.

ANGEL FOOD

Sift one cup of pastry flour once, then measure and sift three times.
Add a pinch of salt to the whites of eight or nine eggs or just one cup of whites, beat about one-half, add one-half teaspoon of cream of tartar, then beat the whites until they will stand of their own weight; add one and one-fourth cups of sugar, then flour, not by stirring but folding over and over until thoroughly mixed in; flavor with one-half teaspoon of vanilla or almond extract. Bake in an ungreased pan, patent tube pan preferred. Place the cake in an oven that will just warm it enough through until the batter has raised to the top of the mold, then increase the heat gradually until the cake is well browned over; if by pressing the top of the cake with the finger it will spring back without leaving the imprint of the finger the cake is done through. Great care should be taken that the oven is not too hot to begin with as the cake will rise too fast and settle or fall in the baking. Bake thirty-five to forty minutes. When done, invert the pan; when cool remove from pan.

SUNSHINE CAKE

Beat yolks of five eggs lightly, add one teaspoon of vanilla, or grated rind of one lemon. In another bowl beat seven whites to a froth with a scant one-half teaspoon of cream of tartar, then beat until whites are very stiff. Gradually add one cup of granulated sugar, sifted three times, to the beaten whites. Fold whites and sugar, when beaten, into the beaten yolks. Sift one cup of flour three times, then put into sifter and shake lightly, fold into the cake. Bake forty minutes in ungreased cake pan. As directed for sponge cake invert pan. Remove cake when it has cooled.

MOCHA TORTS

Beat one cup of powdered sugar with the yolks of four eggs; when very light, add one cup of sifted flour in which has been mixed one teaspoon of baking-powder, add three tablespoons of cold water, one-half teaspoon of vanilla, one tablespoon essence of mocha, add the stiffly-beaten whites and bake fifteen to twenty minutes in two layer pans in a moderate oven. Spread when cold with one-half pint of cream to which has been added one tablespoon of mocha essence, one and one-half tablespoon of powdered sugar and then well whipped. Garnish with pounded almonds.

PEACH SHORTCAKE

Make a sponge cake batter of four eggs, one cup of pulverized sugar, a pinch of salt and one cup of flour. Beat the eggs with the sugar until very light. Beat until the consistency of dough and add the grated peel of a lemon, and last the sifted flour. No baking-powder necessary. Bake in jelly tins. Cut the peaches quite fine and sugar bountifully. Put between layers. Eat with cream.

The same recipe may be used for Strawberry Shortcake.

BREMEN APPLE TORTE

Take seven peeled and cored apples, six tablespoons of sugar, two tablespoons of butter, and cook together until apples are soft. Cream six eggs; add to them one pint of sour cream, one tablespoon of vanilla, one-half teaspoon of cinnamon, and sugar to taste; then pour into the cooked apples and let all boil together till thick. Remove from stove.
Take three cups of finely rolled zwieback, and in the bottom of a well-greased pan put a layer of two cups of crumbs, then a layer of the apple mixture, a layer of the remaining crumbs, and lastly lumps of butter over all. Bake one hour.

VIENNA PRATER CAKE

Cream the yolks of six eggs with one cup of granulated sugar. Add three-fourths cup of sifted chocolate, three-fourths cup of flour (sifted twice), one and one-half teaspoon of vanilla. Add the beaten whites. Bake thirty minutes. When cold; cut in half and fill with the following: One cup of milk, yolks of two eggs, one cup of chopped walnuts. Boil, stirring constantly to prevent curdling. Sweeten to taste, and after removing from the fire add one tablespoon of rum.
Spread while hot.

SAND TORTE

Cream one-half pound of butter with one-half pound of sugar; drop in, one at a time, the yolks of six eggs. Add one small wine glass of rum, one-fourth pound of corn-starch, and one-fourth pound of flour that have been thoroughly mixed; one teaspoon of baking-powder, the beaten whites of six eggs. Bake one hour in a moderate oven.

ALMOND CAKE OR MANDEL TORTE, No. 1

Take one-half pound of almonds and blanch by pouring boiling water over them, and pound in a mortar or grate on grater (the latter is best).
Beat yolks of eight eggs vigorously with one cup of sugar, add one-half lemon, grated peel and juice, one tablespoon of brandy, and four lady-fingers grated, the almonds, and fold in the stiffly-beaten whites of eggs. Bake in moderate oven one hour.

ALMOND CAKE OR MANDEL TORTE, No. 2

Take one-fourth pound of sweet almonds and one-eighth pound of bitter ones mixed. Blanch them the day previous to using and then grate or pound them as fine as powder. Beat until light the yolks of nine eggs with eight tablespoons of granulated sugar. Add the grated peel of one lemon and one-half teaspoon of mace or vanilla. Beat long and steadily.
Add the grated almonds and continue the stirring in one direction. Add the juice of the lemon to the stiff-beaten whites. Grate four stale lady fingers, add and bake slowly for one hour at least.

BROD TORTE

Take six eggs, seven tablespoons of granulated sugar, seven tablespoons of bread crumbs, one-eighth pound of chopped almonds, one-half teaspoon of allspice, one tablespoon of jelly, grated rind and juice of one lemon, one teaspoon of cinnamon, one-half teaspoon of cloves, one-half wine glass of brandy. Beat yolks of eggs well and add sugar and beat until it blisters, add bread crumbs, almonds, jelly, spice, lemon, and brandy. Then add beaten whites, and bake slowly about forty minutes.

RYE BREAD TORTE

Beat the yolks of four eggs very light with one cup of sugar; add one cup of sifted dry rye bread crumbs to which one teaspoon of baking-powder and a pinch of salt have been added. Moisten one-half cup of ground almonds with two tablespoons of sherry, add and lastly fold in the beaten whites of eggs. Bake in ungreased form in moderate oven.

ZWIEBACK TORTE

Beat the yolks of six eggs with one and one-eighth cups of sugar, add one-half box of zwieback, which has been rolled very fine, add one teaspoon of baking-powder, season with one tablespoon of rum or sherry wine and one-half teaspoon of bitter almond extract. Lastly fold in the stiffly-beaten whites of the six eggs and bake in ungreased form in moderate oven three-quarters of an hour.

CHOCOLATE BROD TORTE

Separate the yolks and whites of ten eggs. Beat the yolks with two cups of pulverized sugar. When thick add one and three-fourth cups of sifted dry rye bread crumbs, one-half pound of sweet almonds, also some bitter ones, grated or powdered as fine as possible, one-fourth pound of citron shredded fine, one cake of chocolate grated, the grated peel of one lemon, the juice of one orange and one lemon, one tablespoon of cinnamon, one teaspoon of allspice, one-half teaspoon of cloves, and a wine glass of brandy. Bake very slowly in ungreased form. Frost with a chocolate icing, made as follows:

Melt a small piece of chocolate. Beat the white of an egg stiff with scant cup of sugar, and stir into the melted chocolate and spread with a knife.

BURNT ALMOND TORTE

Beat up four eggs with one cup of sifted powdered sugar. Beat until it looks like a heavy batter. When you think you cannot possibly beat any longer stir one cup of sifted flour with one-half teaspoon of baking-powder. Stir it into batter gradually and lightly, adding three tablespoons of water. Bake in jelly tins. Filling: Scald one-fourth pound of almonds (by pouring boiling water over them), remove skins, put them on a pie plate and set them in the oven to brown slightly.

Meanwhile, melt three tablespoons of white sugar, without adding water, stirring it all the while. Stir up the almonds in this, then remove them from the fire and lay on a platter separately to cool. Make an icing of the whites of three eggs beaten very stiff, with one pound of pulverized sugar, and flavor with rose-water. Spread this upon layers and cover each layer with almonds. When finished frost the whole cake, decorating with almonds.

CHOCOLATE TORTE

Take nine eggs, one-half pound of pulverized sugar, one-half pound of almonds, half cut and grated; one-half pound of finest vanilla chocolate grated, one-half pound of raisins, cut and seeded; seven soda crackers, rolled to a powder; one teaspoon of baking-powder, juice of three lemons and one-fourth glass of wine. Beat whites of eggs to a stiff froth and stir in last. Beat yolks with sugar until very light; then add chocolate, and proceed as with other torten.

DATE TORTE

Beat one-half pound of pulverized sugar with the yolks of six large eggs. Beat long and steadily until a thick batter. Add one-half pound of dates, cut very fine, one teaspoon each of allspice and ground cinnamon, one-fourth pound of chocolate grated, juice and peel of one lemon, three and one-half soda crackers, rolled to a fine powder, one teaspoon of baking-powder, and last the stiff-beaten whites. Bake slowly. Cake can be cut in half and put together with jelly.

GERMAN HAZELNUT TORTE

Beat together for twenty minutes until very light the yolks of eight eggs with one-half pound of granulated sugar, then add the very stiffly-beaten whites of eggs, place the bowl in which it has been stirred over a boiler in which water is boiling on the stove, stir continually but slowly until all the batter is well warmed but not too hot, add a small pinch of salt, and one-half pound of grated hazelnuts, add the nuts gradually, mix well and pour into a greased spring form.
Bake very slowly. The grated rind of one-half lemon can be added if desired. Ice with boiled icing.

LINZER TORTE

Cream one pound of butter with one pound of sugar until foamy, then add one by one four whole eggs. Mix well, then stir in three-fourths pound of pounded almonds or walnuts, one teaspoon of cinnamon, one-fourth teaspoon of cloves, one pound of flour, one teaspoon of baking-powder, and a few drops of bitter almond essence. Put in four layer pans and bake in slow oven. Put together with apricot, strawberry, or raspberry jam and pineapple marmalade, each layer having a different preserve. Ice top and sides. If only two layers are desired for home use, half the quantity of ingredients can be used. This is a very fine cake. It is better the second day.

RUSSIAN PUNCH TORTE

Bake three layers of almond tart and flavor it with a wine glass of arrack. When baked, scrape part of the cake out of the thickest layer, not disturbing the rim, and reserve these crumbs to add to the following filling: Boil one-half pound of sugar in one-fourth cup of water until it spins a thread. Add to this syrup a wine glass of rum, and the crumbs, and spread over the layers, piling one on top of the other.
Another way to fill this cake is to take some crab-apple jelly or apple marmalade and thin it with a little brandy.

WALNUT TORTE, No. 1

Grate eight ounces of walnuts and eight ounces of blanched almonds. Beat light the yolks of twelve eggs and three-fourths pound of sugar. Add the grated nuts and one-fourth pound of sifted flour, fold in the whites beaten to a stiff froth. Bake in layers and fill with sweetened whipped cream.

WALNUT TORTE, No. 2

Separate the yolks and whites of six eggs, being very careful not to get a particle of the yolks into the whites. Sift one-half pound of granulated sugar into the yolks and beat until thick as batter. Add a pinch of salt to the whites and beat very stiff. Have ready one-fourth pound of grated walnuts, reserve whole pieces for decorating the top of cake. Add the pounded nuts to the beaten yolks, and two tablespoons of grated lady fingers or stale sponge cake. Last add the stiffly-beaten whites of the eggs. Bake in layers and fill with almond or plain icing.

CHESTNUT TORTE

Boil one pound of chestnuts in the shells, peel them while warm, put nuts through potato ricer or colander. Beat well the yolks of six eggs with six tablespoons of sugar, add all the chestnut puree but two or three tablespoons reserved for top of torte, then add three teaspoons of baking-powder and the well-beaten whites of the six eggs; bake in moderate oven fifteen to twenty minutes. Whip one-half pint of cream, add to this the chestnut puree which was reserved, and a little sugar; garnish torte with this mixture. Enough for twelve persons.

NUT HONEY CAKE

Mix two cups of brown sugar, two cups of honey, six egg yolks and beat them thoroughly. Sift together three cups of flour, one-quarter teaspoon of salt, three teaspoons of ground cinnamon, one-half teaspoon each of ground cloves, ground nutmeg and allspice, and one and one-half teaspoons of soda; add one cup of chopped raisins, one-half ounce of citron cut in small pieces, one-half ounce of candied orange peel cut in small pieces, one-half pound of almonds coarsely chopped. Beat the whites of three eggs very stiff and add them last. Pour the dough to the depth of about half an inch into well-buttered tins and bake in a slow oven for one-half hour.

ICINGS AND FILLINGS FOR CAKES

BOILED ICING

One cup of sugar, one-third cup of boiling water, white of one egg beaten stiff. Pour water on sugar until dissolved, heat slowly to boiling point without stirring; boil until syrup will thread when dropped from tip of spoon; as soon as it threads, pour slowly over beaten white, then beat with heavy wire spoon until of proper consistency to spread. Flavor.

WHITE CARAMEL ICING

Put on to boil two cups of brown sugar, one cup of milk and a small lump of butter. Boil until it gets as thick as cream, then beat with a fork or egg whip until thick and creamy. Spread quickly on cake.

MAPLE SUGAR ICING

Boil two cups of maple sugar with one-half cup of boiling water until it threads from the spoon. Pour it upon the beaten whites of two eggs and beat until cold. Spread between layers and on top of cake. Do not make icings on cloudy or rainy days.

UNBOILED ICING

Take the white of one egg and add to it the same quantity of water (measure in an egg shell). Stir into this as much confectioner's sugar to make it of the right consistency to spread upon the cake. Flavor with any flavoring desired. You may color it as you would boiled frosting by adding fruit coloring.

COCOANUT ICING

Mix cocoanut with the unboiled icing. If you desire to spread it between the cakes, scatter more cocoanut over and between the layers.

NUT ICING

Mix any quantity of finely chopped nuts into any quantity of cream icing (unboiled) as in the foregoing recipes. Ice the top of cake with plain icing, and lay the halves of walnuts on top.

ORANGE ICING

Grate the peel of one-half orange, mix with two tablespoons of orange juice and one tablespoon of lemon juice and let stand fifteen minutes.
Strain and add to the beaten yolk of one egg. Stir in enough powdered sugar to make it the right consistency to spread upon the cake.

CHOCOLATE GLAZING

Grate two sticks of bitter chocolate, add five tablespoons of powdered sugar and three tablespoons of boiling water. Put on the stove, over moderate fire, stir while boiling until smooth, glossy and thick. Spread at once on cake and set aside to harden.

CHOCOLATE ICING, UNBOILED

Beat the whites of three eggs and one and one-half cups of pulverized sugar, added gradually while beating. Beat until very thick, then add four tablespoons of grated chocolate and two teaspoons of vanilla.

This quantity is sufficient for a very large cake.

INSTANTANEOUS FROSTING

To the white of an unbeaten egg add one and one-fourth cups of pulverized sugar and stir until smooth. Add three drops of rose-water, ten of vanilla, and the juice of half a lemon. It will at once become very white, and will harden in five or six minutes.

PLAIN FROSTING

To one cup of confectioner's sugar add some liquid, either milk or water, to make it the right consistency to spread, flavor with vanilla.
Instead of the water or milk, orange juice can be used. A little of the rind must be added. Lemon juice can be substituted in place of vanilla.

Chocolate melted over hot water and added to the sugar and water makes a nice chocolate icing; flavor with vanilla.

ALMOND ICING

Take the whites of two eggs and one-half pound of sweet almonds, which should be blanched, dried and grated or pounded to a paste. Beat the whites of the eggs, add half a pound of confectioner's sugar, one tablespoon at a time, until all is used, and then add the almonds and a few drops of rosewater. Spread between or on top of cake. Put on thick, and when nearly dry cover with a plain icing. If the cakes are well dredged with a little flour after baking, and then carefully wiped before the icing is put on, it will not run and can be spread more smoothly. Put the frosting in the centre of the cake, dip a knife in cold water and spread from the centre toward the edge.

MOCHA FROSTING

One cup of pulverized sugar into which sift two dessertspoons of dry cocoa, two tablespoons of strong hot coffee in which is melted a piece of butter the size of a walnut. Beat well and add a little vanilla.

MARSHMALLOW FILLING

Melt one-half pound marshmallows over hot water, cook together one cup of sugar and one-quarter cup of cold water until it threads thoroughly.
Beat up the white of an egg and syrup and mix, then add to the melted marshmallows and beat until creamy and cool. Can be used for cake filling or spread between two cookies.

FIG FILLING

One pound of figs chopped fine, one cup of water, one-half cup of sugar; cook all together until soft and smooth.

BANANA FILLING

Mash six bananas, add juice of one lemon and three or more tablespoons of sugar; or add mashed bananas with whipped cream or boiled icing.

CREAM FILLING

Scald two cups of milk. Mix together three-fourths of a cup of sugar, one-third cup of flour and one-eighth teaspoon of salt. Add to three slightly-beaten eggs and pour in scalded milk. Cook twenty minutes over boiling water, stirring constantly until thickened. Cool and flavor.
This can be used as a foundation for most fillings, by adding melted chocolate, nuts, fruits, etc.

COFFEE FILLING

Put three cups of warmed-over or freshly made coffee in a small casserole, add two tablespoons of powdered sugar, one-half teaspoon of vanilla. When at boiling point (do not let it boil), add one cup of milk or cream. Then add one tablespoon of cornstarch which has been moistened with cold water. Stir in while cooking till it is smooth and glossy.
When the cake is cool, pour mixture over the layers.

LEMON JELLY FOR LAYER CAKE

Take one pound of sugar, yolks of eight eggs with two whole ones, the juice of five large lemons, the grated peel of two, and one-quarter pound of butter. Put the sugar, lemon and butter into saucepan and melt over a gentle fire. When all is dissolved, stir in the eggs which have been beaten, stir rapidly until it is thick as honey, and spread some of this between the layers of cake. Pack the remainder in jelly glasses.

LEMON PEEL

Keep a wide-mouthed bottle of brandy in which to throw lemon peel. Often you will have use for the juice of lemons only. Then it will be economical to put the lemon peel in the bottle to use for flavoring. A teaspoon of this is sufficient for the largest cake.

LEMON EXTRACT

Take the peel of half a dozen lemons and put in alcohol the same as for vanilla.

VANILLA EXTRACT

Take two ounces of vanilla bean and one of tonka. Soak the tonka in warm water until the skin can be rubbed off; then cut or chop in small pieces and put in two wine bottles. Fill with half alcohol, half water; cork, seal, and in a week's time will be ready for use.

PIES AND PASTRY

PUFF PASTE OR BLAETTER TEIG

To make good puff paste one must have all the ingredients cold. Use a marble slab if possible and avoid making the paste on a warm, damp day.
It should be made in a cool place as it is necessary to keep the paste cold during the whole time of preparation. This recipe makes two pies or four crusts, and requires one-half pound of butter and one-half teaspoon of salt, one-half pound of flour and one-fourth to one-half cup of ice-water.

Cut off one-third of the butter and put the remaining two-thirds in a bowl of ice-water. Divide this into four equal parts; pat each into a thin sheet and set them away on ice. Mix and sift flour and salt; rub the reserved butter into it and make as stiff as possible with ice-water. Dust the slab with flour; turn the paste upon it; knead for one minute, then stand it on ice for five minutes. Roll the cold paste into a square sheet about one-third of an inch thick; place the cold batter in the centre and fold the paste over it, first from the sides and then the ends, keeping the shape square and folding so that the butter is completely covered and cannot escape through any cracks as it is rolled. Roll out to one-fourth inch thickness, keeping the square shape and folding as before, but without butter. Continue rolling and folding, enclosing a sheet of butter at every alternate folding until all four sheets are used. Then turn the folded side down and roll in one direction into a long narrow strip, keeping the edges as straight as possible. Fold the paste over, making three even layers. Then roll again and fold as before. Repeat the process until the dough has had six turns. Cut into the desired shapes and place on the ice for twenty minutes or longer before putting in the oven.

If during the making the paste sticks to the board or pin, remove it immediately and stand it on the ice until thoroughly chilled. Scrape the board clean; rub with a dry cloth and dust with fresh flour before trying again. Use as little flour as possible in rolling, but use enough to keep the paste dry. Roll with a light, even, long stroke in every direction, but never work the rolling-pin back and forth as that movement toughens the paste and breaks the bubbles of air.

The baking of puff paste is almost as important as the rolling, and the oven must be very hot, with the greatest heat at the bottom, so that the paste will rise before it browns. If the paste should begin to scorch, open the drafts at once and cool the temperature by placing a pan of ice-water in the oven.

FLEISCHIG PIE CRUST

For shortening; use drippings and mix with goose, duck or chicken fat.
In the fall and winter, when poultry is plentiful and fat, save all drippings of poultry fat for pie-crust. If you have neither, use rendered beef fat.

Take one-half cup of shortening, one and one-half cups of flour. Sifted pastry flour is best. If you have none at hand take two tablespoons of flour off each cup after sifting; add a pinch of salt. With two knives cut the fat into the sifted flour until the shortening is in pieces as small as peas. Then pour in six or eight tablespoons of cold water; in summer use ice-water; work with the knife until well mixed (never use the hand). Flour a board or marble slab, roll the dough out thin, sprinkle with a little flour and put dabs of soft drippings here and there, fold the dough over and roll out thin again and spread with fat and sprinkle with flour, repeat this and then roll out not too thin and line a pie-plate with this dough. Always cut dough for lower crust a little larger than the upper dough and do not stretch the dough when lining pie-pan or plate.

If fruit is to be used for the filling, brush over top of the dough with white of egg slightly beaten, or sprinkle with one tablespoon of bread crumbs to prevent the dough from becoming soggy.

Put in the filling, brush over the edge of pastry with cold water, lay the second round of paste loosely over the filling; press the edges together lightly, and trim, if needed. Cut several slits in the top crust or prick it with a fork before putting it in place.

Bake from thirty-five to forty-five minutes until crust is a nice brown.

A gas stove is more satisfactory for baking pies than a coal stove as pies require the greatest heat at the bottom.

The recipe given above makes two crusts. Bake pies having a cooked filling in a quick oven and those with an uncooked filling in a moderate oven. Let pies cool upon plates on which they were made because slipping them onto cold plates develops moisture which always destroys the crispness of the lower crust.

TO MAKE AND BAKE A MERINGUE

To beat and bake a meringue have cold, fresh eggs, beat the whites until frothy; add to each white one level tablespoon of powdered sugar. Beat until so stiff that it can be cut with a knife. Spread on the pie and bake with, the oven door open until a rich golden brown. Too much sugar causes a meringue to liquefy; if not baked long enough the same effect is produced.

PIE CRUST (MERBERTEIG)

Rub one cup of butter to a cream, add four cups of sifted flour, a pinch of salt and a tablespoon of brown sugar; work these together until the flour looks like sand, then take the yolk of an egg, a wine-glass of brandy, one-half cup of ice-water and work it into the flour lightly. Do not use the hands; knead with a knife or wooden spoon, knead as little as possible. If the dough is of the right consistency no flour will be required when rolling out the dough. If it is necessary to use flour use as little as possible. Work quickly, handle dough as little as possible and bake in a hot oven. Follow directions given with Fleischig Pie Crust. Fat may be substituted for butter in the above recipe.

PARVE, COOKIE AND PIE DOUGH

Sift into a mixing-bowl one and one-half cups of flour and one-half teaspoon of baking-powder. Make a depression in the centre; into this pour a generous half cup of oil and an exact half cup of very cold (or ice) water; add pinch of salt, mix quickly with a fork, divide in two portions; do not knead, but roll on a well-floured board, spread on pans, fill and bake at once in a quick oven.

No failure is possible if the formula is accurately followed and these things observed; ingredients cold, no kneading or re-rolling; dough must not stand, but the whole process must be completed as rapidly as possible.

Do not pinch or crimp the edge of this or any other pie. To do so makes a hard edge that no one cares to eat. Instead, trim the edges in the usual way, then place the palms of the hand on opposite sides of the pie and raise the dough until the edges stand straight up. This prevents all leakage and the crust is tender to the last morsel.

TARTLETS

Roll puff paste one-eighth of an inch thick; cut it into squares; turn the points together into the middle and press slightly to make them stay. Bake until thoroughly done; place a spoonful of jam in the centre of each; cover the jam with meringue and brown the meringue in a quick oven.

By brushing the top of the paste with beaten egg, diluted with one teaspoon of water, a glazed appearance may be obtained.

BANBURY TARTS

Cut one cup of seeded muscatel raisins and one cup of nuts in small pieces, add one cup of sugar, one well-beaten egg, one tablespoon of water, the juice and grated rind of one lemon. Mix well. Line patty-pans with pie dough, fill with mixture and bake until crust is brown.

FRUIT TARTLETS

If canned fruit is used, take a large can of any kind of fruit, drain all the syrup off and put in a saucepan with an equal quantity of sugar.
Cook until it forms a syrup, then pour in the fruit, which has been stoned (if necessary), and cook until the whole is a syrupy mass.

If fresh fruit is used, put on two parts of sugar to one of water and cook until syrupy, then add the fruit, which has been peeled, sliced and stoned, and cook until the whole is a thick, syrupy mass.

Line the patty cases or plain muffin rings with the puff paste. Put a spoonful or two of the fruit in each one and bake a nice brown. Peaches, white cherries, Malaga grapes, huckleberries and apples make nice tartlets.

One large can California fruit fills twelve tartlets.

APPLE FLADEN (HUNGARIAN)

Rub together on a pastry-board one-half pound of sweet butter with one pound (four cups sifted) of flour, add four tablespoons of powdered sugar, a little salt, four egg yolks and moisten with one-half cup of sour cream; cover and set aside in the ice-box for one-half hour. Take two pounds of sour apples, peel, cut fine, mix with one-half cup of light-colored raisins, sugar and cinnamon to taste. Cut the dough in two pieces, roll out one piece and place on greased baking-pan, spread over this four tablespoons of bread crumbs and the chopped sugared apples, roll out the other half of dough, place on top and spread with white of one egg, sprinkle with two tablespoons of powdered almonds. Bake in hot oven.

LINSER TART

Make a dough of one-half pound each of flour, sugar and almonds that are grated with peel on, two eggs, a little allspice, a little citron, pinch of salt. Flavor with brandy. Take a little more than half, roll it out and line a pie-pan, put strawberry jam on and then cut rest of dough in strips and cover the same as you would prune pie. Brush these strips with yolk of egg and bake in moderate oven.

MACAROON TARTS

Line a gem or muffin-pan with rich pie dough; half fill each tart with any desired preserve, and bake in a quick oven. Beat the whites of three eggs to a stiff froth and add one-half pound of powdered sugar and stir about ten minutes or until very light, and gradually one-half pound of grated almonds. Divide this macaroon paste into equal portions. Roll and shape into strips, dusting hands with powdered sugar in place of flour.

Place these strips on the baked tarts in parallel rows to cross each other diagonally. Return to oven and bake in a slow oven about fifteen minutes. Let remain in pans until almost cold.

LEMON TART (FLEISCHIG)

Make a rich crust and bake in small spring form. Beat three whole eggs and yolks of three very light with one cup of sugar. Add juice of three lemons and grated rind of one, and juice of one orange. Put whole on stove and stir until it comes to a boil. Put on baked crust, spread a meringue made of the remaining three whites and three tablespoons of sugar on top, and put in oven to brown. May be used as a filling for tartlets.

VIENNA PASTRY FOR KIPFEL

Take one-half pound of pot cheese and one-half pound of butter and two cups of flour sifted four times, add a pinch of salt and work these ingredients into a dough; make thirty small balls of it and put on a platter on the ice overnight. In the morning roll each ball separately into two-inch squares. These squares may be filled with, a teaspoon of jelly put in the centre and the squares folded over like an envelop; or fill them with one-half pound of walnuts, ground; one-half cup of sugar and moisten with a little hot milk. Roll and twist into shape. Brush with beaten egg and bake in a moderately hot oven.

CHEESE STRAWS

One-half cup of flour, two tablespoons of butter, four tablespoons of grated cheese, yolk of one egg, dash of cayenne pepper, enough ice-water to moisten. Mix as little as possible. Roll out about a quarter of an inch thick and cut into long, narrow strips. Shake a little more cheese on top and bake in hot oven. This is also an excellent pie crust for one pie, omitting pepper and cheese.

Serve cheese straws with salads.

LAMPLICH

Make a mince-meat by chopping finely eight medium-sized apples, one-half pound each of raisins, currants and sugar, a little citron peel, two or three cloves and one teaspoon of powdered cinnamon.

Cut some good puff paste into little triangles and fill with the mince, turning the corners of the paste over it so as to make little puffs.
Place these closely together and on a buttered baking-dish until it is full. Now mix two tablespoons of melted butter with one teacup of thick syrup flavored with essence of lemon, and pour it over the puffs. Bake until done in a rather slow oven.

MIRLITIOUS

Pound and sift six macaroons; add one tablespoon of grated chocolate and one pint of hot milk. Let stand ten minutes, and then add yolks of three eggs well beaten, one tablespoon of sugar, one teaspoon of vanilla. Line patty-tins with puff paste; fill with the mixture and bake twenty minutes.

APPLE PIE, No. 1

Pare, core and slice four apples. Line a pie-plate with plain pastry.
Sprinkle with bread crumbs. Lay in the apples, sprinkle with one-half cup of sugar, flavor with cinnamon, nutmeg or lemon juice or two tablespoons of water if apples are not juicy. Cover with upper crust, slash and prick and bake in moderate oven until the crust is brown and the fruit is soft.

APPLE PIE, No. 2

Put in saucepan one-half cup of sugar and one-fourth cup of water, let it boil a few minutes, then lay in five large apples or six small ones, which have previously been peeled and quartered; cover with a lid and steam until tender but not broken. Line pie-plate with rich milchig pastry, lay on the apples, sprinkle with sugar and cinnamon and bits of butter drop a few drops of syrup over all and bake.

INDIVIDUAL APPLE DUMPLINGS

Butter six muffin rings and set them on a shallow agate pan which has been well buttered. Fill the rings with sliced apples. Make a dough of one and one-half cups of pastry flour sifted several times with one-half teaspoon of salt and three level teaspoons of baking-powder. Chop into the dry ingredients one-fourth of a cup of shortening, gradually add three-fourths of a cup of milk or water. Drop the dough on the apples on the rings. Let bake about twenty minutes. With a spatula remove each dumpling from the ring, place on dish with the crust side down. Serve with cream and sugar, hard sauce or with a fruit sauce.

WHIPPED CREAM PIE

Make a crust as rich as possible and line a deep tin. Bake quickly in a hot oven and spread it with a layer of jelly or jam. Next whip one cup of sweet cream until it is thick. Set the cream in a bowl of ice while whipping. Sweeten slightly and flavor with vanilla, spread this over the pie and put in a cool place until wanted.

GRATED APPLE PIE

Line a pie-plate with a rich puff paste. Pare and grate four or five large tart apples into a bowl into which you have stirred the yolks of two eggs with about half a cup of sugar. Add a few raisins, a few currants, a few pounded almonds, a pinch of ground cinnamon, and the grated peel of a lemon. Have no top crust. Bake in a quick oven. In the meantime, make a meringue of the whites of the eggs by beating them to a very stiff froth and add about three tablespoons of pulverized sugar.
Spread this over the pie when baked and set back in the oven until brown. Eat cold.

APPLE CUSTARD PIE

Line your pie-plates with a rich crust. Slice apples thin, half fill your plates and pour over them a custard made of four eggs and two cups of milk, sweetened and seasoned to taste.

CHERRY PIE, No. 1

Line a pie-plate with rich paste, sprinkle cornstarch lightly over the bottom crust and fill with cherries and regulate the quantity of sugar you scatter over them by their sweetness. Bake with an upper crust, secure the edges well by pinching firmly together. Eat cold.

CHERRY PIE, No. 2

Pick the stems out of your cherries and put them in an earthen crock, then set them in the oven until they get hot. Take them out and seed them. Make tarts with or without tops and sugar to your taste. The heating of the fruit gives the flavor of the seed, which is very rich, but the seeding of them while hot is not a delightful job. Made this way they need no water for juice.

SNOWBALLS

Pare and core nice large baking apples, fill the holes with some preserves or jam, roil the apples in sugar and cover with a rich pie crust and bake. When done, cover with a boiled icing and set back in the oven, leaving both doors open to let the icing dry.

BLACKBERRY AND CURRANT PIE

When ready to make the pie, mix as much fruit in a bowl as required, sweeten, stirring the sugar through the berries and currants lightly with a spoon. Dust in a little flour and stir it through the fruit. Cut one of the pieces of pastry in halves, dust the pastry-board with flour and roll the lump of pastry out very thin, cover the pie-plate, a big deep one, with the pastry, trim off the edges with a knife, cutting from you. Fill the dish with the fruit, dust the surface well with flour.
Roll out the other piece for the top crust, fold it over the rolling pin, cut a few gashes in it for a steam vent.

Carefully put on the top crust, trim it well about the edge of the pie-plate. Press it closely together with the end of your thumb or with a pastry knife and stand the pie in a moderate oven and bake till the surface is a delicate brown. Then remove the pie and let it stand until it is cool.

The top crust may be made lattice fashion by cutting the pastry in strips, but it will not be as good as between two closed crusts.

CUSTARD PIE

Line the pie-plate with a rich crust. Beat up four eggs light with one-half cup of sugar, a pinch of salt, one pint of milk and grated nutmeg or grated lemon peel, and pour in shell and bake in slow oven.

CREAM PIE

First line a pie-plate with puff paste and bake, and then make a cream of the yolks of four eggs, a little more than a pint of milk, one tablespoon of cornstarch and four tablespoons of sugar, and flavor with two teaspoons of vanilla. Pour on crust and bake; beat up the whites with two tablespoons of powdered sugar and half a teaspoon of cream of tartar. Spread on top of pie and set back in the oven until baked a light brown.

COCOANUT PIE

Line a pie-plate with puff paste and fill with the following custard: Butter size of an egg, creamed with one cup of granulated sugar, one tablespoon of flour, three-fourths cup of grated cocoanut, one tablespoon of milk, vanilla, pinch of salt, and the beaten whites of three eggs.

COCOANUT LEMON PIE

Beat the yolks of six eggs and one cup of sugar until very light, squeeze in the juice of three lemons and the rind of two of them, stir well, then add one-half of a cocoanut grated, and lastly add the whites of six eggs, beaten to a stiff froth. Line a deep pie-plate with rich pastry, sprinkle a little flour over it, pour in the lemon mixture and bake. This makes one pie in deep pie-plate.

LEMON PIE, No. 1

Cover the reverse side of a deep pie-plate with a rich puff paste, and bake a light brown. Remove from the oven until the filling is prepared.
Take a large juicy lemon, grate and peel and squeeze out every drop of juice. Now take the lemon and put it into a cup of boiling water to extract every particle of juice. Put the cup of water on to boil with the lemon juice and grated peel, and a cup of sugar; beat up the yolks of four eggs very light and add to this gradually the boiling lemon juice. Return to the kettle and boil. Then wet a teaspoon of cornstarch with a very little cold water, and add also a teaspoon of butter and when the boiling mixture has thickened remove from the fire and let it cool. Beat up the whites of the eggs to a very stiff froth, add half of the froth to the lemon mixture and reserve the other half for the top of the pie. Bake the lemon cream in the baked pie-crust. Add a few tablespoons of powdered sugar and half a teaspoon of cream of tartar to the remaining beaten whites. If you desire to have the meringue extra thick, add the whites of one or more eggs. When the pie is baked take from the oven just long enough to spread the meringue over the top, and set back for two or three minutes, leaving the oven doors open just the least bit, so as not to have it brown too quickly.

LEMON PIE, No. 2

Line a deep pie-plate with nice crust, then prepare a filling as follows: After removing the crust from two slices of bread about two inches thick, pour over it one cup of boiling water; add one dessertspoon of butler, and beat until the bread is well soaked and smooth; then add the juice and rind of one lemon, one cup of sugar, the yolks of two eggs, well beaten, and a little salt; mix well; fill pie with mixture and bake in hot oven until firm. Beat white of two eggs to a stiff froth, add four tablespoons of powdered sugar and spread on top and brown.

MOCK MINCE PIE

Pare, core, and chop fine eight tart apples. Add one cup of seedless raisins, one-half cup of currants, one ounce of chopped citron, one-half teaspoon each of cinnamon, cloves, spice and mace, a tiny bit of salt and grated nutmeg. Pour over whole one tablespoon of brandy, and juice and rind of one lemon. Line bottom and sides of plate with crust, fill in with mixture, and put strips of dough across.

MINCE PIE

Boil two pounds lean, fresh beef. When cold, chop fine. Add one-half pound chopped suet, shredded very fine, and all gristle removed. Mix in a bowl two pounds of seeded raisins, two pounds of currants, one-half pound of citron, chopped very fine. Two tablespoons of cinnamon, two tablespoons of mace, one grated nutmeg, one tablespoon of cloves, allspice, and salt. Mix this with meat and suet. Then take two cups of white wine, two and one-half pounds of brown sugar. Let stand. Chop fine four apples, and add meat to fruits. Then mix wine with whole, stir well, and put up in small stone jars. This will keep all winter in a cool place. Let stand at least two days before using. Line pie-plates with a rich crust, fill with mince meat mixture, put a rich paste crust on top, or strips if preferred, prick slightly and bake. Serve warm, not hot.

PUMPKIN PIE

Press through a sieve one pint of stewed pumpkin, add four eggs and a scant cup of sugar. Beat yolks and sugar together until very thick and add one pint of milk to the beaten eggs. Then add the pressed pumpkin, one-half teaspoon of cinnamon, less than one-half teaspoon of mace and grated nutmeg. Stir the stiffly-beaten whites in last. Bake in a very rich crust without cover.

GRAPE PIE

Squeeze out the pulps and put them in one vessel, the skins into another. Then simmer the pulp a little and press it through a colander to separate the seeds. Then put the skins and pulps together and they are ready for the pies.

HUCKLEBERRY PIE

Line a pie-plate with rich pastry. Pick, clean and wash one pint of huckleberries, drain and lay them thickly on the crust. Sprinkle thickly with sugar, lightly with cinnamon, and drop bits of butter over the top.
Bake a nice even brown.

PEACH CREAM TARTS

One cup of butter, and a little salt; cut through just enough flour to thoroughly mix, a cup of ice-water, one whole egg and the yolks of two eggs mixed with a tablespoon of brown sugar. Add to the flour in which you have previously sifted two teaspoons of baking-powder. Handle the dough as little as possible in mixing. Bake in round rings in a hot oven until a light brown. When baked, sift pulverized sugar over the top and fill the hollow centre with a compote of peaches. Heap whipped cream or ice-cream on top of each one, the latter being preferable.

MOCK CHERRY PIE

Cover the bottom of pie-plate with rich crust; reserve enough for upper crust. For filling use two cups of cranberries, cut in halves; one cup of raisins, cut in pieces; two cups of sugar, butter the size of walnut.
Dredge with flour, sprinkle with water. Bake thirty minutes in a moderate oven.

PEACH CREAM PIE

Line a pie-plate with a rich crust and bake, then fill with a layer of sweetened grated peaches which have had a few pounded peach kernels added to them. Whip one cup of rich cream, sweeten and flavor and spread over the peaches. Set in ice-chest until wanted.

PEACH PIE, No. 1

Line a pie-plate with a rich pie-crust, cover thickly with peaches that have been pared and sliced fine (canned peaches may be used when others are not to be had), adding; sugar and cover with strips of dough; bake quickly.

PEACH PIE, No. 2

Pare, stone, and slice the peaches. Line a deep pie-plate with a rich paste, sprinkle a little flour over the bottom crust and lay in your fruit, sprinkle sugar liberally over them in proportion to their sweetness. Add a few peach kernels, pounded fine, to each pie and bake with crossbars of paste across the top. If you want it extra fine, with the whites of three eggs to a stiff froth and sweeten with about four tablespoons of pulverized sugar, adding one-fourth of a teaspoon of cream tartar, spread over the pie and return to the oven until the meringue is set. Eat cold.

PINEAPPLE PIE, No. 1

Line your pie-plate with a rich paste, slice pineapples as thin as possible, sprinkle sugar over them abundantly and put flakes of sugar here and there. Cover and bake.

You may make pineapple pies according to any of the plain apple pie recipes.

PINEAPPLE PIE, No. 2

Pare and core the pineapple and cut into small slices and sprinkle abundantly with sugar and set it away in a covered dish to draw enough juice to stew the pineapple in. Bake two shells on perforated pie-plates of a rich pie dough. When the pineapple is stewed soft enough to mash, mash it and set it away to cool. When the crust is baked and cool whip half a pint of sweet cream and mix with the pineapple and fill in the baked shell.

PRUNE AND RAISIN PIE

Use one-half pound of prunes, cooked until soft enough to remove the stones. Mash with a fork and add the juice in which they have been cooked; one-half cup of raisins, cooked in a little water for a few minutes until soft; add to the prune mixture with one-half cup of sugar; a little ground clove or lemon juice improves the flavor. Bake with two crusts.

PRUNE PIE

Make a rich pie paste. After the paste is rolled out thin and the pie-plate lined with it, put in a layer of prunes that have been stewed the day before, with the addition of several slices of lemon and no sugar.

Split the prunes in halves and remove the pits before laying them on the pie crust.

After the first layer is in sprinkle it well with sugar, then pour over the sugar three or four tablespoons of the prune juice and dust the surface lightly with flour.

Repeat this process till there are three layers, then cut enough of the paste in strips to cover the top of the fruit with a lattice crust and bake the pie in a rather quick oven.

Few pies can excel this in daintiness of flavor.

PLUM PIE

Select large purple plums, about fifteen plums for a good-sized pie; cut them in halves, remove the kernels and dip each half in flour. Line your pie-tin with a rich paste and lay in the plums, close together, and sprinkle thickly with a whole cup of sugar. Lay strips of paste across the top, into bars, also a strip around the rim, and press all around the edge with a pointed knife or fork, which will make a fancy border.
Sift powdered sugar on top. Damson pie is made in the same way. Eat cold.

RHUBARB PIE

Make a very rich crust, and over the bottom layer sprinkle a large tablespoon of sugar and a good teaspoon of flour. Fill half-full of rhubarb that has been cut up, scatter in one-fourth cup of strawberries or raspberries, sprinkle with more sugar and flour, and then proceed as before. Over the top dot bits of butter and another dusting of flour.
Use a good cup of sugar to a pie. Pinch the crusts together well after wetting them, to prevent the juice, which should be so thick that it does not soak through the lower crust at all, from cooking out.

STRAWBERRY PIE

Make a rich fleischig pie-crust and bake on the reverse side of pie-pan. Pick a quart of berries, wash and drain, then sugar. Take the yolks of four eggs beaten well with one-half cup of sugar and stir the beaten whites gently into this mixture. Pour over strawberries. Put in pie-crust and bake until brown. This mixture with most all fruit pies will be found delicious.

SWEET POTATO PIE

Measure one cup of mashed, boiled sweet potatoes. Thin with one pint of sweet milk. Beat three whole eggs very light with one-half cup of sugar. Mix with sweet potatoes. Season with one-quarter of a nutmeg grated, one teaspoon of cinnamon, and one-half teaspoon of lemon extract. Line pie-plate with crust, fill with mixture, and bake in quick oven.

VINEGAR PIE

Line a pie-plate with a rich crust and fill with the following mixture: One cup of vinegar, two of water and two cups of sugar, boil; add a lump of butter and enough cornstarch to thicken; flavor with lemon essence and put in a shell and bake.

MOHNTORTE

Line a form with a rich puff paste, fill with half a pound of white mohn (poppy seed) which has been previously soaked in milk and then ground. Add a quarter of a pound of sugar and the yolks of six eggs; stir all together in one direction until quite thick. Then stir the beaten whites, to which add two ounces of sifted flour and a quarter of a pound of melted butter. Fill and bake. When done, frost either with vanilla or rose frosting.

RAISIN PIE

Line pie pan with rounds of rich pastry, fill with same mixture as for "Banbury Tarts"; cover with a round of pastry and bake a light brown.

RAISIN AND RHUBARB PIE

Chop one cup of rhubarb and one cup of raisins together, add two tablespoons of melted butter or chicken fat, grated rind and juice of one lemon, one cup of sugar, one well beaten egg, one-quarter cup of bread or cracker crumbs, one-half teaspoon of salt; mix all ingredients thoroughly. Bake between two rounds of pastry. Canned rhubarb may be used.

COOKIES

In baking small cakes and cookies, grease the pans. If the pans cool before you can take off the cookies, set back on stove for a few moments. The cakes will then slip off easily. Sponge, drop cakes, anise cakes, etc., are better baked on floured pans.

A whole raisin, an almond blanched, a piece of citron or half a walnut may be used to decorate.

A good way to glaze is, when cookies are about baked, rub over with a brush dipped in sugar and water and return to oven a moment.

FILLED BUTTER CAKES (DUTCH STUFFED MONKEYS)

Make a paste by working three-fourths pound of butter into one pound of flour, with three-fourths pound of light brown sugar, one egg, one teaspoon of cinnamon, and a pinch of salt.

Next mix one-half pound of finely chopped citron peel with one-half pound of ground almonds, and three ounces of butter. Then flavor with one-half teaspoon of vanilla and bind with the yolks of two eggs.

Roll out the dough and divide into two parts. Place one-half on a well-buttered flat pan and spread the mixture over it and cover with the other half of the paste. Brush with beaten egg, sprinkle with poppy seed and bake in a moderately quick oven for one-half hour. When done let cool and then cut into square or oblong pieces.

The butter cakes may be made of one layer of dough sprinkled with citron and almonds and some poppy seed.

SUGAR COOKIES

In a mixing bowl put a cup of sweet butter and two cups of granulated sugar; beat these ingredients to a cream, then add three eggs, grated lemon rind, and four tablespoons of brandy. Beat the added ingredients thoroughly with the others till the mixture is smooth and creamy. Sift three cups of flour in a big bowl with a teaspoon of salt and three teaspoons of baking-powder; stir this a little at a time in the bowl with the other ingredients, until the mixture is a light dough, just stiff enough to roll out. If there is not enough flour, sift more in to make the dough the desired stiffness; then dust the pastry board well with flour, put part of the dough on the board, toss it lightly with your hands from side to side till the dough is covered with flour. Then dust the rolling-pin well with flour and roll the dough very thin; cut it in shapes with a cookie cutter, lift each cookie up carefully with a pancake turner, slip them quickly in a big baking-pan, the inside of which has been well rubbed with flour, and bake them in a moderate oven till light brown.

Just a moment before taking the pan out of the oven sprinkle the surface of the cookies lightly with granulated sugar. When a little cool take the cookies out of the pan with the pancake turner and lay them on a big platter. When they are cold put the cookies in a stone crock.

It is a good plan to have two or three baking-pans so, while one panful is baking, another may be filled and be ready to put in the oven when the other is removed. Only put enough dough on the pastry board at a time to roll out nicely on it.

OLD-FASHIONED HAMBURGER COOKIES

Take one pound of butter one pound of sugar, yolks of six eggs, hard-boiled, and flour enough to make a dough that is not too stiff.

Dissolve three cents worth of ammonia (hartshorn) in scalded milk. Place the ammonia in a large bowl and pour one cup of scalding milk over it. After this has cooled add it to the dough with one-half cup of cold milk. Flavor to taste. Flour the pans and the cookie dough. Roll and proceed as with sugar cookies.

MOTHER'S DELICIOUS COOKIES (MERBER KUCHEN)

Take ten boiled eggs and two raw ones, one pound of best butter, half a pound of almonds, one lemon, some cinnamon one wineglass of brandy, one pound of pulverized sugar and about one pound and a half of flour. This quantity makes one hundred cookies, and like fruit cake, age improves them, in other words, the older the better. Now to begin with: Set a dish of boiling water on the stove, when it boils hard, break the eggs carefully, one at a time, dropping the whites in a deep porcelain dish, and set away in a cool place. Take each yolk as you break the egg and put it in a half shell, and lay it in the boiling water until you have ten boiling. When boiled hard take them up and lay them on a plate to cool. In the meantime, cream the butter with a pound of pulverized sugar, add the grated peel of a lemon, a teaspoon of cinnamon and half of the almonds, which have been blanched and pounded or grated (reserve the other half for the top of the cookies, which should not be grated, but pounded). Add the hard-boiled yolks, which must be grated, and the two raw eggs, sift in the flour, and add the brandy. Beat up the whites of the twelve eggs very stiff, add half to the dough, reserving the other half, but do not make the dough stiff, as it should be so rich that you can hardly handle it. Flour the baking-board well, roll out about an eighth of an inch thick. Now spread with the reserved whites of eggs, reserving half again, as you will have to roll out at least twice on a large baking-board. Sprinkle well with the pounded almonds after you have spread the beaten whites of the eggs on top, also sugar and cinnamon. Cut with a cookie-cutter. Have at least five large pans greased ready to receive them. See that you have a good fire. Time to bake, five to ten minutes. Pack them away when cold in a stone jar or tin cake-box. These cookies will keep a long time.

VANILLA COOKIES

Rub one cup of butter and one cup of sugar to a cream; add two eggs and two level teaspoons of baking-powder, flour enough to make a dough.

BLANC MANGE

Heat one quart of milk to boiling point. Dissolve four large tablespoons of cornstarch in a quarter cup of cold milk. Beat two whole eggs with one-half cup of sugar until light, and add a tiny pinch of salt. When the milk begins to boil, add a piece of butter, size of a hickory nut, then pour it over the well-beaten eggs and sugar, mix well, and put back on the stove. Stir until it begins to boil, then stir in the dissolved cornstarch until the custard is very thick. Remove from the fire, flavor with vanilla or lemon, pour into a mold, and set on ice till very cold and firm. Serve with cream.

FLOATING ISLAND

Beat light the yolks of three eggs with one-quarter cup of sugar. Scald a pint of milk, beat up the whites of three eggs very stiff and put them into the boiling milk, a spoonful at a time. Take out the boiled whites and lay them on a platter; now pour the hot milk gradually on the beaten yolks, when thoroughly mixed, return to the fire to boil. When it begins to thicken remove. When cool, flavor with vanilla or bitter almond. Pour into a deep glass dish; put the whites on top, and garnish with jelly or candied fruit. Eat cold.

RED RASPBERRY OR CURRANT FLOAT

Take a half-pint glass of red raspberry or currant juice and mix it with a quarter cup of sugar. Beat the whites of four eggs to a stiff froth and add gradually a quarter cup of powdered sugar. Press the raspberries through a strainer to avoid seeds and by degrees beat the juice with the sugar and eggs until so stiff that it stands in peaks. Chill it thoroughly and serve in a glass dish half filled with cold whipped cream. Heap on the mixture by the spoonful, like floating island. If currant juice is used it will require a pint of sugar.

www.ingramcontent.com/pod-product-compliance
Lightning Source LLC
Chambersburg PA
CBHW081726100526
44591CB00016B/2523